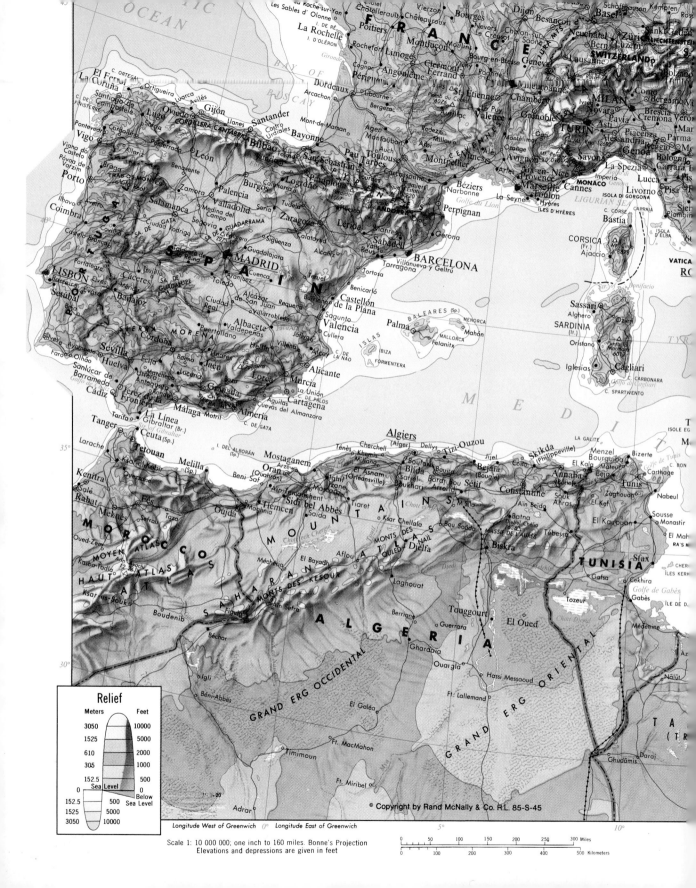

ATLANTIC OCEAN

BAY OF BISCAY

FRANCE

SWITZERLAND

SPAIN

PORTUGAL

LISBON

MADRID

BARCELONA

CORSICA (Fr.)

SARDINIA (It.)

BALEARES (Sp.)

MALLORCA

IBIZA

FORMENTERA

MENORCA

MEDITERRANEAN

LIGURIAN SEA

MOROCCO

ALGERIA

TUNISIA

ATLAS MOUNTAINS

HAUT ATLAS

MOYEN ATLAS

SAHARAN ATLAS

MONTS DES KESOUR

MONTS DES OULED NAIL

GRAND ERG OCCIDENTAL

GRAND ERG ORIENTAL

| Relief | | |
|---|---|---|
| Meters | | Feet |
| 3050 | | 10000 |
| 1525 | | 5000 |
| 610 | | 2000 |
| 305 | | 1000 |
| 152.5 | | 500 |
| 0 | Sea Level | 0 |
| 152.5 | | 500 Below Sea Level |
| 1525 | | 5000 |
| 3050 | | 10000 |

Longitude West of Greenwich 0° Longitude East of Greenwich

Scale 1: 10 000 000; one inch to 160 miles. Bonne's Projection
Elevations and depressions are given in feet

| | 0 | 50 | 100 | 150 | 200 | 250 | 300 Miles |
|---|---|---|---|---|---|---|---|
| 0 | 100 | 200 | 300 | 400 | 500 Kilometers |

# Enchantment of the World

# SPAIN

## By Esther and Wilbur Cross

---

**Consultant:** Ana Maria Vazquez, M.A. in History, University of Fribourg, Fribourg, Switzerland

**Consultant for Reading:** Robert L. Hillerich, Ph.D., Bowling Green State University, Bowling Green, Ohio

CHILDRENS PRESS ®

CHICAGO

*The old quarter of Cuenca*

Library of Congress Cataloging in Publication Data

Cross, Wilbur.
    Spain.

    (Enchantment of the world)
    Includes index.
    Summary: Describes the geography, history, culture,
industry, and people of the varied southern European
country.
    1. Spain—Juvenile literature. [1. Spain]
I. Cross, Esther. II. Title. III. Series.
DP17.C65   1985        946        85-16588
ISBN 0-516-02786-7        AACR2

**Picture Acknowledgments**
**Cameramann International**—9, 15, 51 (left), 70 (bottom),
106 (right)
© **Stuart Cohen**—61 (left), 80 (bottom), 104, 107 (left)
**Colour Library International**—Cover, 4, 16, 17, 22, 46
(bottom), 55, 56, 57 (left), 63 (bottom), 72, 77, 106 (left),
113
© **Victor Englebert**—14, 20, 50, 63 (top left), 65, 70 (top),
102 (right)
© **Robert Frerck/Odyssey Productions, Chicago**—33, 82
(top), 97 (bottom)

**Hillstrom Stock Photo:**
    © **Art Brown**—36, 95
    © **Steven E. Gross**—21, 61 (right), 98 (bottom left)
    © **Jack Lund**—8 (left), 48 (left), 100
    © **Karen I. Hirsch**—66
    © **W. R. Reesman**—49, 107 (right)
    © **William Stenseth**—53, 80 (top)
**Historical Pictures Service, Chicago**—29, 37, 42, 90, 93, 94
**Image Finders:**
    © **Bob Skelly**—6, 19, 74, 86
**Nawrocki Stock Photo:**
    © **Janet Davis**—51 (right), 98 (bottom right), 103 (right)
    © **Ruth Dunbar**—112 (right)
**Chip and Rosa Maria Peterson**—88, 103 (left and middle)
    © **Stephen A. Johnson**—8 (right)
**Roloc Color Slides**—5, 10, 25, 26, 46 (top), 63 (top right),
69, 79, 82 (bottom), 91 (right), 98 (top left and top right),
101, 105 (left), 109 (right), 111
**Root Resources:**
    © **Kenneth Rapalee**—58 (right)
© **M. B. Rosalsky**—109 (left)
**Spanish National Tourist Office**—48 (right), 57 (right), 58
(left), 67, 68, 73, 75 (2 photos), 89, 97 (top), 102 (left), 105
(right), 112 (left)
**Tom Stack and Associates:**
    © **Mickey Gibson**—91 (left)
    © **Gary Milburn**—12
**Stock Imagery/Hillstrom Stock Photo:**
    © **Novak**—30, 35, 40, 45, 84, 85
**United Press International**—44
**Maps by Len Meents**—21, 55, 63, 65
**Courtesy Flag Research Center, Winchester,
Massachusetts 01890:** Flag on back cover
**Cover:** Salobreña, on a rock above a sea of sugarcane

*Dancers at the Seville fair*

TABLE OF CONTENTS

*A deep ravine divides the town of Ronda into two halves.*

# Chapter 1
# *THE NOBLE IMAGE*
# *OF SPAIN*

Spain was once described as being "like a great castle that rises from the sea." A topographical map of Spain shows why this description is so appropriate. The borders of the country are high and rugged like castle walls. In the center of the country lie broad, low tablelands that could easily be the courtyard of an enormous castle. The turrets and inner battlements are the isolated peaks and crags that dot the countryside.

According to a popular legend, when God created Spain its people were granted three wishes. They chose to have the world's most varied climate, the most beautiful women and handsome men, and the most appetizing foods and wines. The Spaniards— and many visitors to this land of Old World enchantment— believe there is a ring of truth in this legend.

There can be no doubt that Spain is rich in beauty and contrasts alike. Spain is "European" and very much a part of the continent. Yet it is also close enough to the north coast of Africa to reflect the influence of some of the oldest and greatest civilizations of the

*Flowered patio in Córdoba (left). Dry central plains (right)*

ancient world. Spain's southernmost tip—the one closest to
Africa—is the region known as Andalusia. Many of the cities here,
like Málaga, Granada, Seville, and Córdoba, are rich in Moorish
architecture. The narrow byways, flower-bedecked patios, and
whitewashed houses are characteristic of Morocco and Algeria.
There are palm trees and groves of tropical fruits and rich
vineyards. And there are the people and costumes that are so
typically Spanish in picture books and art.

A view of Spain is quite different in the central tablelands of
Castile (the "courtyard of the castle"). This is an area of broad
plains, stretching to the horizon on all sides, and is much drier
and browner than the lands to the south. The sweep of the plains
is broken by high sierras and in some places by the ramparts of
medieval castles, the bell towers of ancient monasteries, and the
modern buildings of the great central cities like Madrid, Toledo,
Guadalajara, and Segovia. Scattered throughout these plains are
country villages and a mosaic of pastures and fields.

*Luxuriant green pastures of northern Spain*

The northwestern region of Spain is almost like a different country when compared with the east and the south. It is known as Galicia—a land of lush green hills, woodlands, streams, waterfalls, and pastures that resembles the landscapes of southern Ireland or parts of England. Galicia occupies the northwestern peninsula of Spain, bounded by the Bay of Biscay to the north, the Atlantic Ocean to the west, and Portugal to the south. Much of the coastline here is as rugged as that of the Norwegian fjords, ragged with bays known as *rías,* and dotted with small fishing villages that cling to narrow beaches. The seacoast cities and towns are known for their abundance of seafoods, especially shellfish like lobsters, shrimp, and crabs.

The diversity of these three major regions characterizes the diversity of Spain itself. A well-known Spanish proverb, *Quien dice España dice todo,* sums up the Spaniards' pride in the unique variety to be found in their country: "He who says Spain, says everything." It is certainly true of the flora. Because of the many

*Young dancers of Mallorca, in the Balearic Islands, in native costumes*

variations in climate, Spain has more types of vegetation than any other country in Europe. The variety of trees alone ranges from palms and olive trees along the Mediterranean coast to oaks, chestnuts, elms, and pines along the Atlantic. The dry interior regions are forested with ilex and cork trees and with drought-resistant shrubs and plants much like those in American deserts.

The same kind of diversity is seen in the people, although many will stoutly defend their heritage as being truly "Spanish" and distinct from that of any other nation. The major divisions of Spanish peoples are cultural groups rather than distinct ethnic groups. They include the Castilians of central Spain; the Basques of the northern provinces; the Catalans of the northeast; the Galicians of the far northwest; and the Andalusians of the south.

Politically, the country is divided into fifty provinces, forty-seven of which are on the mainland (often called the Iberian

Peninsula). Two provinces are made up of the Canary Islands, off the west coast of Africa, and one is the Balearic Islands, in the western Mediterranean. Much more important than these administrative divisions, however, are Spain's historical and cultural groups. These have roots in the ancient kingdoms that preceded the modern state. Their centuries-old regional differences and, in some cases, isolation from each other have given Spain myriads of dialects, as well as diverse cultures.

The ancient history of the peoples of the Iberian Peninsula (which also includes neighboring Portugal) has been described as "a hodgepodge of tribal movements, warfare, incursions, invasions, and intermixing of various tribes."

They included waves of Celts from France, Germany, the Scottish Highlands, Wales, and Cornwall; colonists from Greece and Phoenicia; seagoing peoples from North Africa; Romans who crossed the high Pyrenees; and later Visigoths and Vandals from as far east as the Black Sea. It was impossible for such a mixture of peoples to become unified in a matter of a few centuries. However, near the end of the Middle Ages, Spain gradually became united as a country.

Spain's cultural achievements, too, have not only enhanced the lives of native Spaniards, but also influenced Spanish colonies. Literature, music, drama, painting, and the other arts developed broadly with the influence of migrants on the peninsula from the days of the earliest tribesmen to recent times.

In its culture, as well as in its history, geography, environment, and government, Spain echoes the proverb "He who says Spain, says everything." It is the theme that runs through the nation, influencing every part of its past and present, and probably its future as well.

*The Pyrenees Mountains*

## Chapter 2

# *MOUNTAINS, COASTS, AND PLAINS*

Covering more than 190,000 square miles (492,119 square kilometers), or nearly five-sixths of the Iberian Peninsula, mainland Spain is the second largest country in western Europe, and almost four times the size of the state of New York. A little more than 4,000 additional square miles (10,360 square kilometers) are added by the Canary Islands, the Balearic Islands, and five "Places of Sovereignty" along the coast of Morocco. On a flat map, the shape of the country is neither unusual nor memorable, though some say it resembles the hide of a bull stretched to dry in the sun. On a topographical map, however, the sculptured terrain is unique and beautiful.

Much of the perimeter of the country is distinguished by high mountain ranges, rugged outcroppings, cliffs, and magnificent escarpments. Notable is the Pyrenees chain, which runs east and west from the Bay of Biscay to the Mediterranean. The Pyrenees, topped by the 11,168-foot (3,404-meter) Pico de Aneto, serve as a formidable barrier between Spain and France.

*Village in the Cordillera Cantábrica*

## THE GEOGRAPHICAL REGIONS

A geographical tour of Spain reveals it has five principal regions.

*The Cantabrian Zone* includes the Basque provinces, Galicia, and Asturias. This is an area of high, craggy mountains and deep valleys, with many forests, fertile fields, and an abundance of water. Some of the peaks have been described as "nests of eagles" perching in the clouds. There are gaunt outcroppings of granite and volcanic rock formed many centuries ago throughout the Cordillera Cantábrica, or Cantabrian Mountains, which have peaks from 7,000 feet (2,134 meters) to more than 8,500 feet (2,591 meters). Along the Atlantic and the Bay of Biscay, much of the shoreline is made up of high cliffs dropping into the sea, with a backdrop of mountains inland. Transportation in the most mountainous sections is difficult. In one stretch of railroad, for example, there are twenty-two tunnels in 21 miles (34 kilometers).

*Farm town in the Pyrenees region of Navarre*

    *The Pyrenees Zone* lies to the east of the Cantabrian. It features the Pyrenees Mountains, which stretch some 260 miles (418 kilometers) from the Bay of Biscay to the Mediterranean Sea. Although the Pyrenees range is quite narrow, averaging 60 miles (97 kilometers) wide, its central portion is well over 5,000 feet (1,524 meters) high. The entire upland area receives abundant rain and snow. However, much of the water runs off into deep gorges and is difficult to divert for irrigation.

    The provinces of the Pyrenees region are Navarre, Aragon, and Catalonia. Navarre, at the western end, is a land of vast hardwood forests, where the mountain torrents are used to power hydroelectric plants. In Aragon, on the southern slopes of the highest mountains, the land broadens into arid plains drained by the Ebro River. Catalonia has many pine-covered mountains and fertile plains. Since this zone lies along the French border, where invaders have tried to cross into Spain over the centuries, many towns here have monuments and relics of fierce battles.

*Windmills are scattered throughout La Mancha.*

*The Meseta and the Interior Zone* make up almost half of the mainland of Spain. This vast central plateau sits at an elevation of 2,000 to 2,500 feet (610 to 762 meters). The terrain is flat for the most part, is generally arid and somewhat barren, and can be extremely hot in the summer months.

The Castilian tableland was the center of life for the ancient kingdoms of León, Old Castile, New Castile, and La Mancha. Much of the countryside is as little populated today as it was centuries ago. The houses of isolated villages and towns seem to huddle together, and the communities are separated by vast stretches of desolate plains.

*The Andalusian Zone,* to the south, includes the cities of Seville, Córdoba, and Granada. Along the Mediterranean, it has stretches of coastal plain with many beaches and inlets. Inland, it consists of rolling hills, fertile valleys, and tall mountains, some of which are almost permanently capped with snow. The climate is

*Acres of olive groves
in the Andalusian lowlands*

distinctly Mediterranean in the Andalusian lowlands, where it is
common to see palm trees, bougainvillea, fields of tobacco and
sugarcane, or olive groves. Winters are mild and sometimes rainy;
summers are sunny, dry, and usually hot. The most changeable
weather conditions occur in the spring and fall, when cloudbursts
drop torrents of rain over only small areas at a time.

*The Levant* is the east coast along the Mediterranean Sea. It runs
from Valencia south to Alicante and Murcia, ending near Almería
and Cape Gata. The southeastern seacoast of Spain is known as
the Costa Blanca ("white coast"), where the mountains come right
down to the sea. In the southern section, particularly, are
numerous fine, white beaches, resort areas, and harbors, one of
the best being at Cartagena.

Known as the "rice bin" of Spain, the Levant is the source of
much of the rice eaten in Spain, as well as its famous Valencia
oranges and other citrus fruits. These crops depend almost

entirely upon irrigation. The regions where they are grown lack the necessary rainfall, and water has to be transported from distant streams and mountain cascades. The most essential feature for agriculture along the Levantine coast is the dependable abundance of sunshine.

## THE RIVERS OF SPAIN

Spain has some eighteen hundred rivers and streams, but most of them are less than 50 miles (80.5 kilometers) long and are only rocky beds during the dry season. Only two major rivers in Spain are more than 550 miles (885 kilometers) long—the Tagus, which cuts through the heart of the central Meseta, and the Ebro, which parallels the Pyrenees in the northeast. Many attempts have been made to use these rivers and streams for irrigation in the more parched regions of the country. But the problem has always been the great variation in the flow of most of the rivers, ranging from floods during rainy seasons to complete evaporation during dry periods.

The Tagus, almost 600 miles (965 kilometers) long, has its origins in the Sierra de Gudar in eastern Spain. It drains the central plateau as it heads westward, crossing into Portugal and eventually emptying into the Atlantic Ocean in a broad estuary. For a short distance, it forms part of the Spanish-Portuguese border. Not far from where it rises in the mountains, the Tagus passes Toledo and irrigates crops in the Meseta. The Tagus is navigable for less than 100 miles (161 kilometers) of its length. However, since it passes through deep gorges where it is broken by waterfalls, it has great potential for hydroelectric power.

The Ebro River collects most of its water from the Cantabrian

*A modern hydroelectric plant beneath the medieval walls of Avila*

Mountains and from small tributaries in Aragon, Catalonia, and Navarre as it flows southeastward between the Pyrenees and the Iberian mountain ranges. It empties through a broad delta into the Mediterranean Sea south of Tarragona. Navigation on the Ebro is severely restricted, not only because of seasonal variations in the river's flow, but because of the many irrigation canals built along it. Almost half of Spain's hydroelectric power is supplied by plants along the Ebro.

Other important rivers are the Duero, the Guadiana, and the Guadalquivir. The Guadalquivir has been called the country's "most valuable river." It rises in southeastern Spain and flows southwestward into the Gulf of Cádiz. Although it is only 350 miles (563 kilometers) long, it is fed constantly by tributaries. It is navigable for oceangoing vessels as far as Seville, some 50 miles upstream, making that city Spain's only major inland river port.

Most of the other rivers in Spain are characteristically short, local in character, and updependable for irrigation. Along the entire Mediterranean coast from Barcelona south, for example, the

*Sparse pine trees in the rocky soil of León province*

typical stream is almost bone dry for a large part of the year. But streambeds that are nothing but a trickle can become raging torrents during brief periods of rain or sudden melting of snow.

## NATURAL RESOURCES AND VEGETATION

Although Spain is noted for extensive regions that are arid and sparse, it has a variety of natural vegetation and regions of rich, fertile soils. During the last glacial period, or Ice Age, about ten thousand years ago, lower plains were covered with grasses and forests. Alpine vegetation was prominent in the uplands. But when primitive tribes began cutting down the forests, the change upset the balance of nature. The climate actually became warmer and drier, the forests receded to the north and northwest, and the alpine vegetation disappeared from all but the higher mountains.

Even more damaging to the once-fertile plains was the growth of scrubby bushes that tended to replace the forestlands and push

*Red clay soil in the Meseta is hard to cultivate.*

them even farther back. The cork, juniper, and wild olive trees that once flourished over much of the Iberian Peninsula can be found only in more isolated regions and along the coast.

One of the most serious problems affecting tree farming and the growing of crops has been the soil condition. Coarse-grained soil, often lacking in organic matter, predominates throughout Spain. Many of the highlands, such as the Cantabrian Mountains, the Pyrenees, and the Sierra Nevada, are composed of silt, sand, gravel, and other materials that lack soil nutrients. Even in the lowlands, plants can barely live in the silty sands. As little as 10 percent of the country has finer-grained soils suitable for agriculture, and even these tend to have a clay, or clay-and-sand, base. Unfortunately, some of the richest soils are in regions that are arid and require broad irrigation, or else in salty marshlands, as in the lower valley of the Guadalquivir River. Some of the farmlands of the Meseta suffer from the presence of *calveros*. (Calvero comes from the word *calvo,* which means "bald.") These

*The dramatic, rocky coast of Mallorca*

are barren stretches that are eroded, with loose rock fragments scattered over land that was once rich. Some soils, too, contain acids and salts that restrict plant growth.

## THE BALEARIC AND CANARY ISLANDS

Off the east coast of Spain in the Mediterranean Sea lie the Balearic Islands, which form the Baleares province of the country. Lying between fifty and two hundred miles (80.5 and 322 kilometers) off the coast, the sixteen islands of this group are of special geological interest. They are actually a continuation of the Sierra Nevada mountain range of southern Spain, which in prehistoric times extended out into the sea. Their surfaces are hilly and undulating, and they are composed of the same types of limestones found in the mountains from which they separated millions of years ago. Unlike the mainland, however, their surface soils are excellent for trees, decorative plants, and crops, which thrive in the warm winters and sunny summers. The mountains are forested. Fruits, especially olives and grapes, are grown here, as well as wheat and vegetables.

The four most important islands in the group are Mallorca, Menorca, Ibiza, and Formentera. Mallorca is 60 miles (96.5 kilometers) long, shaped somewhat like an Indian arrowhead, and covers 1,405 square miles (3,639 square kilometers). The topography of the island is dramatic, largely because of the Tramuntana range on the north and west coasts, which has nine peaks higher than 3,000 feet (914 meters) and one that rises to almost 5,000 feet (1,524 meters). The mountains, acting as a windbreak, protect the central plain, known as *Es Pla*, where the weather conditions are so favorable and the soil so rich that farmers can harvest four crops of grain in a single year!

By contrast, Menorca is small (only 271 square miles [702 square kilometers]), with a coastline broken up by more than 120 bays and coves. Menorca is relatively flat along its perimeter, and hilly in the center. The highest elevation, Monte Toro, however, is barely over 1,000 feet (305 meters). Stretching out around it, like a huge patchwork quilt, are cultivated fields and pastures. Here some forty thousand head of cattle produce milk that makes Mahoin cheese world famous. In addition to cheese, the chief products are wine, grains, olives, and flax. Fishing and the growing of livestock for export are also important to the island's economy.

The main town, Mahon, is noted for a natural harbor, three-and-a-half miles long, that is one of the finest in the world. The typical sauce from Mahon is *mahonesa*, which has become the familiar mayonnaise sauce.

The island of Ibiza, slightly smaller than Menorca, is a land of rolling, pine-clad hills, fertile valleys, and deep inlets and coves. One of its major features is the town of Ibiza, an ancient seaport, which still has very narrow, cobbled streets and an inner, walled citadel that dates back to the days of the Greeks and Phoenicians. In tiny inland villages, like Santa Gertrudis and Santa Inés, many of the local farmers still dress and till their fields as they did a century ago. In addition to farmland, which requires terraces and irrigation, the island contains fisheries and saltworks.

The tiny island of Formentera, barely ten miles to the south of Ibiza and connected to it by ferry, is linked geographically and politically to Ibiza. However, it is remote and less populated.

The other important Spanish islands are the Canary Islands, a group of seven with a total land area of just over 2,800 square miles (7,252 square kilometers). They form an archipelago in the Atlantic Ocean some 65 miles (105 kilometers) off the northwest coast of Africa. They constitute two provinces of Spain. The first is Grand Canary, which includes Grand Canary, Lanzarote, and Fuerteventura islands. The second is Tenerife, which includes the islands of Tenerife, La Palma, Gomera, and Hierro. All the islands are of volcanic origin and are still subject to eruptions and earthquakes. As a result they are rugged, with high peaks and steep, rocky terrain. Mount Teide on Tenerife rises 12,162 feet (3,707 meters), the highest point in all of Spain—and even more impressive since it occupies an island of less than 800 square miles (2,072 square kilometers). Often snowcapped, Mount Teide looks over the port of Santa Cruz and broad stretches of evergreen forest.

Since they lie roughly on the same latitude as Florida, all of the Canary Islands enjoy a warm climate, with a mean temperature of

*Banana plantation near Las Palmas in the Canary Islands*

68 degrees Fahrenheit (20 degrees Celsius). But each island is different in topography, vegetation, and even way of life.

There is some dispute over the origin of the islands' name. "Canary" is said to have originated from the Latin *canis*, meaning "dog," because of packs of wild dogs seen on the islands by early Roman explorers. Later, the islands became known for the wild canaries that lived in the forests and were later tamed and bred for bird-lovers around the world. The birds took their name from the islands—not the other way around.

The most important islands besides Tenerife are Fuerteventura, in the shape of a whale; Grand Canary, sometimes referred to as "a continent in miniature" because of its variety of landscapes ranging from jungles to deserts; Lanzarote, which in some places resembles the surface of the moon and has geothermal heat beneath its surface; and La Palma, which has the largest volcanic crater yet discovered, with a rim 17 miles (27.3 kilometers) in circumference.

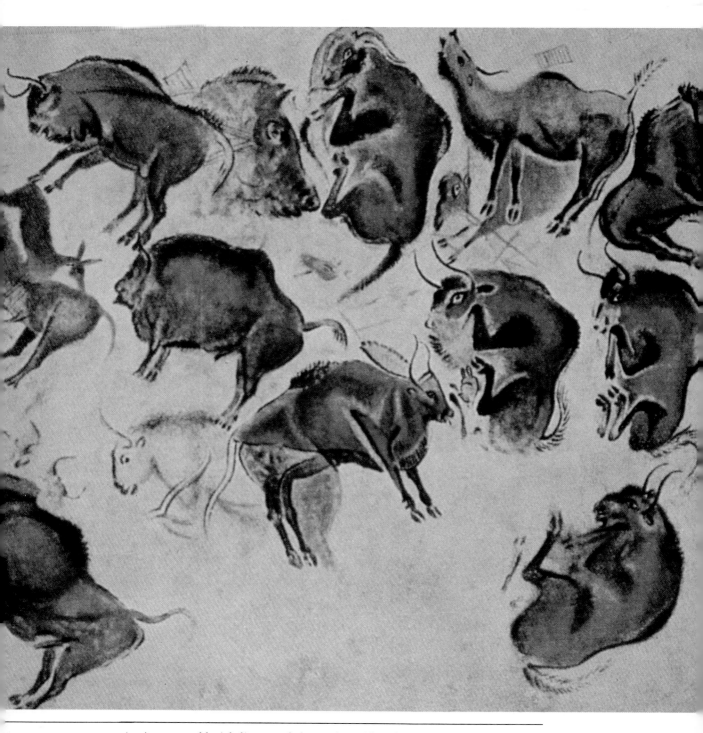

*A nine-year-old girl discovered the ancient Altamira cave paintings in 1879.*

# Chapter 3

# THE CONQUERORS
# AND THE CONQUERED

Almost twenty thousand years ago, members of an unknown primitive tribe, living near what would later be called the Cantabrian Sea, decorated the walls of a cave with sketches. Today those drawings are considered one of the most amazing discoveries in the history of art. The Altamira caves, only a few miles from the city of Santander on the north coast, symbolize Spain's unique artistic and historical heritage. They are by no means isolated examples. The entire Iberian Peninsula, which Spain shares with Portugal, reflects thousands of years of mankind's creativity and genius. Spain's art, like its history, reflects the influence of many peoples and races who have left behind their indelible influence.

## THE IBERIANS

How did it all begin?

As early as 3000 B.C., a race of adventuresome peoples the Greeks called "Iberians" migrated to a region along the Ebro River in what is now northeastern Spain. Their origins are vague, but it is known that they possessed some of the metalworking skills of eastern Mediterranean artisans, as well as some of their farming methods. These Iberian settlers tended to live in tightly knit groups, isolated from each other and not really unified as a nation. Instead, they were more like tribes, with family and regional identity, and often battled with other groups who crossed their paths.

The Iberians built walled cities, some remains of which exist today, were superb horsemen, and were quite artistic, as shown by some small bronze figures that have been unearthed. The most important of the Iberian city-states was Tartessos, which flourished in the fifth and sixth centuries B.C. and was well known to the Greeks. The Greek historian Herodotus wrote about the Iberians and spoke of them as proficient in mining and processing silver, gold, and other metals.

The first important origins of Spain lie in the invasions by the Celts who crossed the Pyrenees in two major waves, first in the ninth century B.C. and again 250 years later. The Celts, a Nordic race, began to mix with the Iberians in the north and in the central plains, forming the Celtiberians. They were largely farmers and herders, although they left behind many examples of their metalworking skills. Their culture exerted a great influence on Spain, even many centuries later.

While these developments were taking place inland, the Greeks, Phoenicians, and Carthaginians were competing for control of the coastline along the western Mediterranean. The Phoenicians had played a part in the founding of Cádiz (known then as Gades) at the southwestern tip of Spain. Although the date has never been firmly established, Cádiz may well be the oldest city in all of

*Hannibal, the Carthaginian general, crossing the Alps to invade Italy in the Second Punic War*

western Europe. Phoenician adventurers and navigators used Cádiz as a base for venturing far out into the Atlantic and for exploring the west coast of Africa.

## LATER CONQUESTS

In the third century B.C., defeated by the Romans in the First Punic War, the Carthaginians tried to rebuild their empire by establishing possessions in Spain. They conquered most of the Iberian Peninsula, and their famous general, Hannibal, used the country as a base for his epic invasion of Italy during the Second Punic War. However, the Carthaginians again met defeat at the hands of the Romans and had to relinquish most of their gains. During this period the Romans used much of Spain as a training ground for their army.

*The legendary Santiago (Saint James) battling the Moors*

An important event occurred, according to tradition, when Saint James brought Christianity to Roman Spain. Saint James later became the patron saint of Spain, under the name of Santiago (Sant Iago).

Although Spain was not yet a political entity, the Romans called it Hispania. It was divided into three provinces and later into nine, each governed separately. Yet under the Romans there was a common bond of law, language, and communication that united the land's many segments. For four hundred years the country was part of the great Roman Empire. Romans and natives alike worked together, played a mutual part in government, and intermarried. They laid out the new cities of Valencia and Mérida in the central plains and Zaragoza in the northeast, and improved many of the existing cities and towns. On this foundation Spain itself would be built. Many communities were enhanced by

Roman aqueducts, theaters, arenas, and public baths. The country was held together by a network of Roman roads, including the noted Via Augusta, which extended all the way across the Iberian Peninsula.

The economy expanded as agriculture was developed and the country became a vast supplier of grains, wool, olive oil, fruits, lumber, and other commodities. As for language, the Latin of the Romans began changing markedly as it was influenced by local usage. Eventually a series of regional Spanish dialects emerged. As the country began to produce writers, they in turn played a part in forming the Spanish language as we know it today.

An abrupt change took place in Spain's history at the very beginning of the fifth century. In the year 405, the Vandals and the Suevi crossed the Rhine River in Germany and began ravaging Gaul, the lands north of the Pyrenees. They were then forced westward into Spain by another Germanic tribe, the Visigoths. The Vandals, who were barbaric and brutal, were eventually pushed southward into Andalusia (originally called *Vandalusia*). There they clung for a time before their enemies forced them across the Strait of Gibraltar to North Africa.

The Visigoths selected Toledo as their capital. On a granite bluff overlooking the Tagus River and protected on three sides by steep gorges, it was a likely citadel. Toledo was to become important from a religious viewpoint, too, as the administrative capital of the Catholic church and the site of several important church councils. But the Visigoth occupation was not a "barbaric invasion," as it has sometimes been called. Rather, the Visigoth kings received imperial commissions to rule the country in the name of the Roman emperor. Their cultural influence was temporary and never of great importance.

# AL-ANDALUS

In the summer of the year 710, a North African military officer and some four hundred soldiers crossed the eight-mile strait between North Africa and the Iberian continent. Small though this force was, it accomplished its objective: to survey the coast and determine the strength of the Visigoth defenses. One year later, after several such scouting raids, a force of between seven thousand and twelve thousand men crossed the same strait in boats in the dark of night. They were Moors, led by Tariq ibn Zayid, who caught the Visigoths off guard and quickly marched inland. At the time, the Visigoth army was fighting off an invasion of Basques near the Pyrenees, far to the north. After the general of the Visigoths, King Roderick, died in battle, Spain was left without a leader and was a much easier prey to invasion.

By the year 718, Spain was completely under the domination of the Moors. They were to rule all of Spain for about three centuries, and for much longer in some parts. Their last stronghold was Granada.

The Moors called the Iberian Peninsula *Al-Andalus*, a name that has continued to this day in Andalusia, where the Moorish influence was greatest. The spreading tide of Islam, the religious faith of the Moors, engulfed the loosely-knit feudal culture that existed under the Romans and Visigoths. The new culture had a great influence on the people of Spain. It affected not only religion, but also architecture, art, medicine, customs, and the whole way of life of the people. Cities like Granada, Seville, and Córdoba became major cultural centers for the Moorish empire, especially in the regions closest to North Africa.

Because many of the Arab invaders were aristocrats with a long

*A twelfth-century depiction of the invading Moors*

heritage of leadership, some Spanish noblemen converted to Islam in order to retain their privileged positions in society. For a time, there was nothing in the rest of Europe to compare with the wealth, power, and culture of Spain under the Moors. The country became noted around the world for its Cordovan leather, Toledo steel, fine silks, and rich wools.

All this was to change, however, for two reasons. The first was internal strife among the leaders of the Moors. It was difficult for the old-line Arabs to maintain peaceful relationships with the new converts to the Islamic religion. The second reason was the resistance to the Moors by certain groups who resented their domination. As early as the middle of the eighth century, there were active movements in the north, especially in Castile and Aragon, to rid Spain of the Moors. This was the start of a crusade that was to last seven hundred years and end with the *Reconquista*, or reconquest of Spain.

By the tenth century, natives had established strongholds in the north along much of the Ebro River. At first, the fortified defenses and the troops that manned them simply blocked the Moors' attempts to push far beyond the central region. Castile ("Land of Castles") became symbolic of this resistance movement. Then the pendulum began to swing and the defenders became aggressors, pushing farther and farther southwestward as they forced the Moors to relinquish their grip on Spain. Within three hundred years, the forces in Aragon had moved halfway down the east coast, along the Mediterranean. An important victory was the seizure of the Mediterranean city of Valencia by James I—known as "The Conqueror"—who defeated the Moorish ruler there. Another great victory was the conquest of Toledo at the end of the eleventh century and its reestablishment as a major seat of Christianity.

## THE GOLDEN AGE

Despite these steady advances against the Moors, Spain suffered greatly from internal strife, largely because of political ambitions and rivalry. One of the most positive and steadying events in medieval Spanish history was the wedding of two royal cousins, Isabella of Castile and Ferdinand of Aragon, in 1469. The marriage unified and strengthened the regions of Castile and Aragon in a vital alliance.

A second event leading to what history would call the Golden Age of Spain was the discovery of America by Christopher Columbus, sailing under the flag of Ferdinand and Isabella. It was not only his discovery but also what it symbolized that brought new recognition to Spain and saw the end of the Moorish

*Ferdinand and Isabella at the reconquest of Granada*

occupation. With the capture of Granada, the last Moorish stronghold in the Iberian Peninsula, Spain could turn to colonization, which made it one of the most important nations of Europe. Now the country was in a position to attempt conquests far beyond its borders.

At the height of this Golden Age, with discoveries of gold and silver in the New World and an alliance (through a royal marriage) with the Hapsburgs of Austria, Spain became the most powerful nation in the Old World. Spain's empire included not only the Iberian Peninsula, but Austria, Belgium, Germany, Holland, Sicily, and large parts of Italy, as well as scattered Mediterranean lands. King Ferdinand was once described as "one of the most skillful diplomats in an age of great diplomats." Queen Isabella was a forceful monarch who was criticized for suppressing faiths other than her own, but who helped Spain to maintain its position of leadership in the Christian world.

*The Spanish Inquisition used religion for political purposes.*

Spain, like other European countries during the Protestant Reformation, persecuted those not belonging to the state religion. This was done to achieve a better political unity and strength. In Spain, as in other countries, one of the most infamous institutions was the much-feared Inquisition, authorized by the church but controlled by the government. It began as a rather straightforward program to determine the sincerity of converted Christians. But it ended with mass expulsions from the country, the punishment of "disbelievers," and in some cases even torture.

This persecution was partly offset by Spain's notable achievements in the New World. Núñez de Balboa reached the Pacific Ocean in 1513 and Ferdinand Magellan's expedition completed the circumnavigation of the globe in 1522. As Cortés, Pizarro, and other conquistadors won victories throughout the New World, the land claimed in the name of Spain became twenty or thirty times the size of Spain itself.

*Destruction of the Spanish Armada*

One of the greatest enemies of Spain during the sixteenth century was England, which also was establishing colonies in the New World. In 1588, King Philip II of Spain launched a large fleet of ships with the intention of invading England, overthrowing Queen Elizabeth, and establishing himself on the English throne. Just as this supposedly "invincible" force was ready to sail, the daring English admiral Sir Francis Drake made a surprise raid on Spain. He led a small force of ships right into the harbor of Cádiz and "singed the beard of the Spanish king." This naturally infuriated Philip, who gave the order for his fleet, called the Armada, to head for England. In a series of sea battles, the Spanish fleet was scattered by the British into the North Sea. Spain lost more than half the ships in the fleet, as well as two-thirds of the sailors. However, this was mainly due to heavy storms the fleet encountered on the way back to Spain.

# DECLINING FORTUNES

Although the defeat of the Spanish Armada was not as quick, decisive, or catastrophic as history books sometimes make it seem, it nevertheless marked a turning point in Spanish history. Internal strife and power struggles between Castilians, Aragonese, and other groups weakened the structure of Spain. Much of the wealth that came from the colonies in the form of precious metals, gems, and other natural resources was squandered on ships, arms, and other military expenditures.

Because of extensive military commitments, the Spaniards placed heavy taxes on the production of manufactured goods, thus pricing them too high for the competitive European market. As domestic production declined, the Spanish people had to rely more and more on costly imports, which weakened the economy even more.

The seventeenth century was a period of economic, military, political, and social decline. Spain's treasury became more and more depleted. There was a fifty-year period of intermittent warfare with France. The people were wasted by a series of plagues and famines, and the land by alternating floods and droughts.

By the eighteenth century, Spain was ruled by the Bourbon dynasty and was strongly influenced by the French. The "Family Compact" was a series of three agreements (1733, 1743, and 1761) between the French and Spanish branches of the Bourbon family. These pacts provided that Spain would support France against the English during the Seven Years' War.

Spain and France, though united by the Family Compact, were defeated by England in 1763 at the end of this war. The defeat strengthened the British control of colonies in North America, since France lost many of its New World colonies and Spain lost Florida to England. This was one of the events that led up to the American Revolution and the formation of the United States in 1776.

Spain, eager to contribute to the downfall of the British in America, actively supported the thirteen colonies in their fight for freedom. An editorial in one of Madrid's leading newspapers, *El Mercurio Histórico,* said in January, 1776: "Everything would appear to make their resistance sacred and worthy of respect and their demands just." Spain is said to have supplied twelve thousand muskets for the Americans in Boston, thirty thousand uniforms, eighty thousand blankets, sixty thousand pairs of boots, and gear for three thousand horses. Spain also opened a number of ports to American warships, where they could get supplies or hide safely from British ships. These ports included Havana, San Juan, New Orleans, Bilbao, and La Coruña.

Because of these actions, England declared war on Spain in 1779, a short conflict ended by the Treaty of Versailles four years later. Spain recovered Florida, as well as the small island of Menorca, but was unable to take Gibraltar even after a two-year siege. Gibraltar remains a British colony to this day.

During the next few years, a complex struggle for power ensued among Spain, France, and England. The outcome was that Spain lost its Trinidad colony to England, lost Louisiana to the French, failed in a second attempt to seize Gibraltar, and had its fleet destroyed by the British off Cape Trafalgar on the southwestern Spanish coast.

As if these setbacks were not devastating enough, the French armies of Napoleon Bonaparte invaded Spain in 1808 and forced

*Napoleon Bonaparte takes over Madrid.*

King Carlos IV to abdicate. Spain suffered what has been called
"her greatest humiliation" when Joseph Bonaparte, Napoleon's
brother, was proclaimed king of Spain. However, not all
Spaniards were greatly humiliated. Many were pro-French,
particularly a small group of high-ranking, influential Spaniards
who called themselves the *afrancesados*.

Hoping to assure the support of this group and also to attract
other Spanish backers, Joseph Bonaparte dissolved certain
religious institutions. His actions only angered many Spaniards,
who fought small, hard-pitched battles in the rural areas and hills
and gradually wore down their French opponents. The citizens of

Zaragoza held out against superior French forces for more than a year. Resistance fighters in the province of Asturias won back much of the land originally lost to the enemy. An army of underground soldiers in Madrid forced the French to abandon that city, at least temporarily. Spaniards were not fighting the Napoleonic Wars but their own war of independence.

Napoleon's troops were eventually defeated by the guerrilla forces and a British army under the Duke of Wellington. Wellington defeated the French conclusively in a battle at Vitoria, near the Pyrenees, ending the Peninsular War. In 1814 Ferdinand VII was restored to the Spanish throne, but was unable to cope with the country's many problems. Spanish colonies in the Americas took advantage of the weakening government to proclaim their independence. Most succeeded.

The middle of the nineteenth century was marred by many internal disorders. Don Carlos claimed the throne after his brother, Ferdinand VII, died and was to be succeeded by his niece, Isabella II. The split in the royal family also divided the nation, which became embroiled in a civil war between the "Carlists" and those who opposed them. For six years, from 1833 to 1839, the Carlists resisted government attempts to subdue them. After that a shaky peace existed, broken by periodic uprisings.

Spain's fortunes reached a low point at the end of the nineteenth century, largely because of the Spanish-American War. It started because Spain was determined to keep Cuba as a colony, whereas many Cubans wanted independence. The situation reached a flash point in 1895, when the move for independence heightened, supported in part by secret backing from groups in the United States. It all came to a head with the mysterious explosion of the United States battleship *Maine*, at anchor in the

*The costly Spanish-American War was a low point in Spain's history.*

harbor at Havana. Calling it an act of aggression by the Spanish military forces in Cuba, and regretting the loss of 260 crewmen, the United States declared war on Spain two months later, in April 1898.

Despite Spain's pledge to defend Cuba "to the last peseta," the Spanish army, weakened after years of fighting the Cuban guerrillas, surrendered after only a few weeks of spotty defense against an American expeditionary force. Even more humbling to the Spaniards was the destruction of their fleet in the Philippines. Admiral George Dewey, the American commander, led a squadron of ships into the harbor of Manila under cover of darkness. By noon the next day, he had destroyed eight Spanish warships, losing only eight of his men during the battle. Spain was forced to relinquish not only Cuba, but Puerto Rico and the Philippines as well.

# THE TWENTIETH CENTURY

The early years of the twentieth century saw Spain unable to recover from its total defeat by the United States. Nationwide despair led several prominent Spaniards to urge their countrymen to accept the fact that Spain was no longer a world power and that its government was out of date. It was time, they said, to take stock of weaknesses and bring about reforms that would "move the nation into the 1900s." This was much easier said than done. Before World War I, it was impossible to form a coalition government the people would support. Many top-ranking leaders initiated movements that seemed to command the necessary backing for brief periods. But all eventually failed.

Spain was neutral in World War I, but staying out of the world-shaking conflict did not solve its problems. The Spanish army was engaged in a long, fruitless conflict in Morocco from 1909 until 1926, where Spain had joined France in trying to set up a government. The Spanish losses were constant and at times heavy, partly because the civilian government in Madrid refused to provide adequate military equipment or financial support. Understandably, efforts to draft soldiers to fight against tribesmen in Morocco sparked strong negative reactions at home.

During the 1920s, the country was under the military dictatorship of General Miguel Primo de Rivera. Although he brought an end to the disastrous war in Morocco, curbed unemployment, and stimulated a temporary financial recovery, his administration was doomed by the oncoming depression. Forced to resign, he died shortly afterwards in exile, leaving Spain in the hands of King Alfonso XIII, who had reigned, in title at least, since 1886.

*Generalissimo Francisco Franco, leader of the Spanish civil war, in a 1970 photo*

In 1931, Alfonso abdicated and the Second Republic was formed. It planned many reforms, but there followed one crisis after another. After a series of controversial elections and political assassinations, part of the army rebelled. Eventually, a group of generals called a *junta* formed a government at Burgos. General Francisco Franco was appointed head of state, with the rank of *generalissimo*.

This rebellion brought about the Spanish civil war, one of the greatest disasters in the history of Spain. It took a huge toll of lives and devastated the land. Worse yet, Spain became a battleground for all of Europe and beyond. Italy and Germany, siding with Franco, sent planes, tanks, and munitions and more than fifty thousand soldiers to aid his cause. On the opposing side, Russia supplied an immense amount of military aid with the sole purpose not of helping Spain, but of exploiting the country for its own political goals. Great Britain and France proposed a nonintervention pact, which was signed by twenty-seven nations.

*King Juan Carlos I*

Ironically, Germany, Italy, and Russia all signed the pact, but had no intention of abiding by it.

The Spanish civil war raged for two-and-a-half years, between 1936 and 1939, leaving more than 600,000 people killed, millions wounded, tens of thousands dead from starvation, and utter devastation across the land. Several hundred thousand Spaniards fled their country, many of them never to return.

The end of the war saw Franco as supreme head of the country, allowing the Fascist Falange to be the only legal political party. His dictatorship continued until his death in November, 1975. In July, 1969, Franco and his government had recognized and designated Prince Juan Carlos as the future king and head of state. Thus it came about that King Juan Carlos I, a descendant of the House of Bourbon, ascended the throne of Spain in 1975. Under him, during the 1980s, the country became a constitutional monarchy, once again promising freedom of expression, freedom of worship, and other basic democratic rights.

*Above: Village women at their spinning wheels*
*Below: Rows of houses in the Castilian village of Aura*

## Chapter 4

# THE PRIDE OF

# COMMUNITY

---

Looking back on the history of Spain, from the time of cavemen to the arrival of Iberians and invasions by various nations and peoples, one feature has always been quite evident: the solidarity of the family and the community. The Spanish people have always held great pride in, and loyalty to, their immediate social and political environment, whether it be a large city, a rural village, or a close-knit region. Changes are taking place, particularly in the large urban areas where it is easy to lose one's sense of identity. Even so, the Spanish people are drawn together by common bonds. A cross-sectional look at some cities, towns, and villages will give an introduction to where, why, and how the Spanish people live.

*Madrid's Plaza de España (left) and the Puerta del Sol (right)*

## A CIVILIZED CAPITAL

Madrid, the capital, is situated in the geographical center of Spain. Madrid has been called "one of the most civilized European capitals." It is populated by some four million people, most of whom are either Spaniards or have adopted Spanish ways. And the Spanish way is to add a dash of *comodidad* ("ease") to one's activities, even in the heart of a great, bustling city.

This leisurely environment is reflected in the city's sense of spaciousness. It can be seen in Madrid's many parks, in the broad, tree-lined avenues, in the traffic circles with their fountains, and in the vistas that look far beyond office buildings and shops. Even the tiniest cafes may have outdoor patios that make patrons feel they are sipping coffee or wine in a much larger environment.

Madrid's city dwellers can drive just thirty to forty miles (48 to 64 kilometers) and reach the open countryside. The city, the highest capital in western Europe, sits on a plateau at an altitude

*Outdoor cafe in Madrid's Plaza Mayor*

of 2,100 feet (640 meters) surrounded by vast plains, mountains, and forests. The region enjoys more cloudless days than do most European cities, with the magnificent blue skies often seen in landscapes of the famous Spanish painter Velázquez. The midday sun in the warm months of the year can be very hot. Perhaps that is why the *Madrileños* (citizens of Madrid) insist on closing shop or leaving work for three hours in the middle of the day for the traditional Spanish siesta.

Another custom, though hardly confined to Madrid, is that of stopping by favorite cafes at the end of the workday to sip coffee or wine. Traditionally, dinner is served after nine, and sometimes as late as midnight, particularly during the summer. Strolling is a pleasant pastime in the evening before dinner or on a Sunday afternoon. Favorite places for this are Retiro Park near the famous Prado Museum of Art, the Botanical Garden, Discovery Square, the Sabatini Gardens, the Plaza de España, and any of the tree-lined streets.

*Many surprises are in store for shoppers at the Rastro.*

There is no end to the types of entertainment and sightseeing available in Madrid. Most popular from early spring until mid-autumn is the bullfight, held in either of two rings in the city. Close runners-up are football (which Americans know as soccer), played in any of several stadiums, and horse racing at Zarzuela Hippodrome.

Another scene of Sunday activity is the *Rastro,* a picturesque flea market where almost every kind of article can be purchased, from inexpensive objects to priceless antiques. The knowledgeable Rastro-goer can pick up a Victorian statue, a collection of old household utensils, a piece of excellent period furniture, dolls from many nations, and even a used costume of a bullfighter.

Madrid is truly a city of contrasts. It boasts some of the tallest, most modern buildings in Europe. It also has its share of narrow, winding streets, lined by whitewashed apartments and shops. The oldest part of Madrid lies in the southwest-central section near the

*Inside the Royal Palace (left). Old Madrid apartments (right)*

Plaza Mayor, one of the loveliest squares in the world. This is the heart of the original city, where plays were performed by roving actors, festivals were celebrated on traditional feast days, and Gypsies sold ornaments and trees during the Christmas season.

Madrid is not considered "old" by Spanish standards. In the tenth century it was a tiny hamlet called Magerit, little more than a cluster of farms on a windswept plain alongside the Manzanares River. King Philip II established his court there in 1561. Then Philip III, who was born in Madrid, made it the permanent capital in 1606, a year after the famous novel *Don Quixote* was published at a little press on Atocha Street. By 1900, it had grown to a city of 300,000 people. Today it has more than four million—large, but not as teeming as many world capitals.

One of the most famous buildings in Madrid, or in all of Spain for that matter, is the Royal Palace. Standing on the site of the former Alcázar, a fortress that burned down in the middle of the eighteenth century, the palace was completed in 1764, during the reign of King Carlos III. It is considered "Bourbon" in style and was the home of the monarchs for more than two centuries.

## LIFE IN A VILLAGE

From one end of Spain to the other lie small villages and hamlets, largely in the rural areas where farming and handicrafts are the chief occupations. One such village is Buendía, 75 miles (121 kilometers) southeast of Madrid in the province of Cuenca. Most of the houses and shops are at the bottom of a valley, clustered around the largest and most prominent building, a seventeenth-century church. Other dominant features near Buendía are the remains of an ancient Roman rampart and a large man-made lake that is used to irrigate the spreading fields.

This picturesque village is a typical rural community where goats, sheep, cows, and pigs are herded along narrow streets, and where people still ride on burros or in creaking donkey carts loaded with wares. The small main road leads in both directions to fields, orchards, and pastures. The grass is sparse and brown during the hot, dry summer months, when even the reservoir and the river are little more than damp collections of rocks and sand.

As in many outlying regions, the villagers speak with accents that foreigners and even Spanish city-dwellers have trouble understanding. Such regional differences in language reflect the centuries of Spanish history when communities were isolated and had little communication with their neighbors.

The pace of life changes very little from day to day in the typical Spanish *aldea* ("village"). In the early morning before sunrise, the sounds of sheep bleating or cattle mooing reveal that farmers and

*Burros still provide transportation in small villages.*

herders are already up and on their way to the fields, some with animals, others with carts. They are not likely to return until sundown. During the day, life in the village is bustling, but never frenzied, as people go about their daily jobs. Women bake bread, sweep their front stoops, or weave baskets and mats. Men of all ages go about their trades, painting walls, repairing trellises, digging irrigation ditches, or replacing roof tiles.

The only real change in the daily routine takes place on Sunday, when the hollow ringing of the church bell announces Mass. The elderly villagers dress in black, the traditional color for churchgoing. Other aspects of life continue though, seven days a week: the crowing of cocks in barnyards, the scurrying packs of dogs seeking discarded food, the endless cooking of native foods on smoky stoves, and the sound of music from inside the whitewashed houses. Always, too, groups of men or women take breaks from their work to enjoy a favorite Spanish diversion: social conversation and gossip.

Jimena de la Frontera is another village, but distinctly different in many ways from Buendía. A brilliant white town a few miles inland from Costa del Sol ("the sun coast") at the southernmost tip of Spain, it perches in the heart of a range of low-lying mountains. The clusters of houses, many of them joined together and sharing common roofs, snake their way around and up a cone-shaped hill, San Cristóbal. At the top sit the still-majestic ruins of a twelfth-century Moorish castle. Its round tower was reconstructed from a fort built by the Romans several hundred years earlier.

This village of some five thousand inhabitants is a kind of crossroads of history. A house here may have Moorish arches, Roman stairways, Spanish balconies, and French antiques. When workers dig to construct patios or gardens, chances are good they will unearth artifacts of an ancient Neolithic tribe.

The Phoenicians, Greeks, and Carthaginians are also thought to have explored the area and made camps and settlements there. It is easy to imagine how they arrived, trudging inland from ships anchored along the shore. Looking south from the stone ramparts of the ruined castle, one can see the sparkling blue of the Mediterranean and the dark, gaunt Rock of Gibraltar, an immense natural landmark for ancient navigators.

Like Buendía and many other Spanish villages, Jimena de la Frontera has its share of donkey carts, cattle, and sheep impeding traffic in the narrow streets. Children in white smocks meander up and down the hill on their way to school. Women work until the evening paseo ("stroll") time arrives and they can visit neighbors.

Mornings and late afternoons are allocated for the heavy work, while the midday siesta is for sipping coffee or wine in the cafes

*Vejer de la Frontera, a typical Andalusian town*

or playing cards or dominoes. The climate in this southern part of Spain varies from mild to hot, and people restrict their activities when the noontime sun floods the village.

## THE SOUTHERN CITIES

Andalusia is the Spain of brilliant foliage, romantic flamenco dances, haunting guitars, and prize horses. It is the land influenced by the architecture and customs of the Romans and Moors. It stretches from the Sierra Morena mountains southward to the Mediterranean Sea. The principal cities of Andalusia are Seville, Málaga, Granada, and Córdoba—each with its distinctive character, history, outlook, and people.

Seville has been described as "the most complete personification of the spirit of Spain" because it reflects so many qualities that are considered typically Spanish. Set like a jewel in the heart of fertile pastures and farmlands, it is also the country's most important

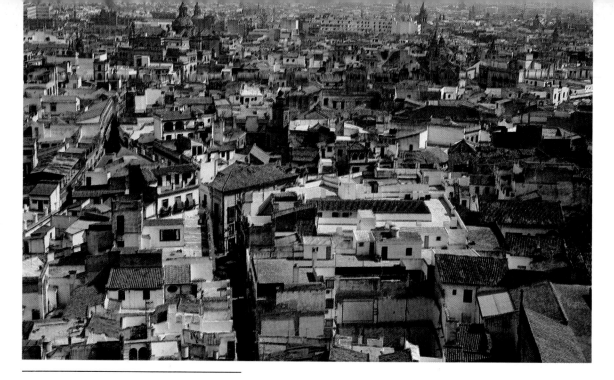

*Overview of Seville's tiled roofs*

western port, even though it lies forty miles (sixty-four kilometers) inland on the Guadalquivir River. It retains an Old World look because its historic buildings have been preserved through the ages, while modern structures have been restricted or constructed to blend in. In a city with many priceless treasures, its architecture is the greatest gem of all. The cathedral, the world's largest Gothic structure and the third largest church in Christianity, sets the style.

Seville was one of the most important cities of Spain when it was reconquered by Ferdinand III in 1248. During the sixteenth century, the city became the headquarters for trade with the New World, outfitting ships that were to sail across the Atlantic and importing goods from the Americas. It is no wonder that the cathedral should be the site of Christopher Columbus's tomb.

The terrain in and around Seville is flat, but the intensely cultivated countryside to the northeast rolls upward along the

*Seville's Plaza de España (left). Córdoba's mosque (right) covers six acres.*

river to the city of Córdoba, ringed by low mountains. This city, too, is dominated by a church—a mosque built by the Moors in the eighth century. Inside there are six hundred columns, linked by horseshoe arches and striped with red and white bricks. The inside is low, only about thirty feet (nine meters) high, but the building extends for 400 feet (122 meters), providing what one visitor called "six acres of barbaric splendor." In the center of the mosque is one of its unique features—a small cathedral built by the Christians after they had expelled the Moslems from Spain.

Of Iberian origin, Córdoba flourished under the Romans before being captured by the Visigoths and later the Moors. In the tenth century, the city was one of the most cultured and sophisticated in all of Europe, known for its great wealth and its artisans who worked with gold, silver, leather, and silk. After that its fortunes declined, but it remains one of the country's most important metropolitan centers.

*Near Granada's magnificent Alhambra (left), Gypsies make their homes in caves (right).*

To the southeast of Seville and Córdoba lies their sister city, Granada. It, too, has a Moorish past that intrigues visitors. The famous Alhambra is an elaborate palace built by Arab rulers on a citadel overlooking the city. Queen Isabella and King Ferdinand are buried together in a double tomb in the Royal Chapel next to the immense cathedral. When their troops captured Granada in 1492, the royal couple earned the title Catholic Sovereigns. And it was here that they launched the final stages of the Reconquest, the military plan to drive the Moslems southward and back to North Africa.

Granada is noted for its Andalusian Gypsies. These are not the nomadic type, who travel from place to place in covered wagons. They are a more stable group who live in town houses and house-caves, particularly on Sacromonte Hill, which is honeycombed with their dwellings. Traditionally, Spanish Gypsies sing and dance the flamenco and wear colorful, flamboyant costumes.

The province of Granada extends south to the Mediterranean area known as Costa del Sol, a sunny region with a subtropical climate. Along the coast are wooded hills that slope down to small coves and secluded beaches, called *calas*. Once sparsely populated, this area has become popular with Spanish vacationers and foreign tourists alike. The province's only port is Motril, although the nearby community of Almuñécar, founded more than three thousand years ago by the Phoenicians, is both a fishing village and a holiday resort.

Southwest of Granada lies the other important Andalusian city, Málaga. It perches on the sea between two steep, imposing mountain ranges. Málaga, a city of almost half a million, is the capital of the Costa del Sol. It is one of the finest Mediterranean ports, where ships export olives, almonds, dried fruits, and the famous Málaga sweet wines.

Here, the noted artist Pablo Picasso was born near the quiet little Plaza de la Merced. Picasso rose from an Old World environment to become one of the greatest geniuses in the field of modern art. The city is famous, too, for its Roman theater, Arabic palace, and a large cathedral known as *La Manquita* ("The One-Armed Lady") because one of its towers was never built. It is said that the funds intended for the missing tower were sent to aid the American colonies during the Revolution.

Founded by the Phoenicians in the twelfth century B.C., Málaga successively passed into the hands of the Carthaginians, the Romans, the Visigoths, and the Moors before finally becoming a medieval Spanish port. The seaport is often called *Málaga la Bella* ("Málaga, the Beautiful") because of its luxuriant flowers and foliage, the mountains and green forests that embrace it, and the verdant countryside in which it is set.

Crowning a hilltop in a setting of cypress, pines, and flowering bougainvillea stands the Moorish Gibralfaro Castle, whose fourteenth-century ramparts overlook the city and the sea. It is matched by the eleventh-century Alcazaba fortress, with lush gardens of honeysuckle, lavender, and jasmine. Facing the city from the sea, visitors are struck by the beauty of the Esplanade, an avenue lined with palm trees and paved with fine mosaic tiles.

## COMMUNITIES OF THE NORTHEASTERN MEDITERRANEAN

The northernmost region of Spain on the Mediterranean is called the Costa Brava ("wild coast"), referring to its jutting rocks and rugged profile. It stretches from the French border south to the little seacoast village of Blanes. Here, pine woods and cork tree groves run down to high, steep cliffs at the edge of the sea. The beaches, narrow pockets of sand walled by jagged rocks, are sometimes inaccessible except from the sea.

The hundreds of sheltered coves made this region the landing point for explorations by the Phoenicians, Greeks, and Romans, who remained long enough to build fortifications and attempt colonization. Forts were necessary in later years, too, when pirates used the isolated harbors to hide from enemy ships. The only real city in this province is its capital, Gerona, with a population of about sixty thousand. Built in pre-Roman times, it lies on the Oñar River. During the Peninsular War its citizens put up heroic resistance against the French.

South of Blanes, the shoreline flattens out into the broad, open beaches of the Costa Dorada ("golden coast"). Here lies Barcelona, the greatest metropolis of the northeast, with over half as many

*Strolling down the* ramblas *in downtown Barcelona (left). Montserrat monastery nestles in the crags of a mountainside near Barcelona (right).*

residents as Madrid itself, making it the second largest city in Spain. It straddles a bay surrounded by mountains, in the midst of which perches the monastery of Montserrat on a wild, rockbound peak.

Despite its size, Barcelona enjoys a relaxed, cosmopolitan atmosphere. Its tree-lined boulevards, street cafes, and parks have been compared with those of Paris. The city is a montage of narrow, cobbled streets, tiny squares with little fountains, patios of every size and shape, bustling waterfronts, and great buildings, old and new. One of the most notable structures is the fourteenth-century cathedral that dominates the Gothic Quarter.

About halfway down the Mediterranean coast is the seaport of Valencia. It developed long ago as an agricultural center and, because of its long dry spells, perfected a sophisticated irrigation system. There was even a *Tribunal de las Aguas* ("water committee") that oversaw the use and distribution of water. The tribunal still meets once a week on the steps of the cathedral.

Valencia is famous for an unusual event, the *Fallas de San José*, which occurs in March. More than 350 sculptured figures are made by competing teams and other groups, depicting people, scenes, or events familiar to Valencian culture or history. A recent one, for example, was a six-story figure of Don Quixote on his horse. The figures are made out of scraps of wood, papier mâché, cloth, and plastic, but some of them cost as much as $25,000 or more! They are erected at intersections and in the plazas during the week-long feast of Saint Joseph that ends on March 19.

This is only one part of what an American writer described as "one of the greatest spectacles of Europe." The old industrial port becomes the center of fireworks displays, costume parades, bullfights, and street-corner cooking contests. The grand finale occurs at midnight on the final day, when every falla figure in the city, from the smallest to those towering several stories high, is set ablaze. Then, as the flaming creatures subside in ashes, the last fireworks are set off, lighting the clear, Valencian sky in all their glory.

South of Valencia lies the Costa Blanca ("white coast"), so named because of the white foam of the Mediterranean, with many fine beaches and clusters of whitewashed towns. Here, the landscape changes from the orange groves of Valencia to tropical vines, olive trees, palms, and almond trees, and summertime lasts most of the year.

Alicante, with almost 300,000 inhabitants, is one of the most popular resorts in Spain. Much of the city and its suburbs have been built in recent years. However, many monuments of the past remain, such as the Castle of Santa Bárbara and Biar Castle, which sit on two high hills, and the parish church of Santa María, built on an ancient Arab mosque.

*Above: Produce market in Valencia (left). Whitewashed town of Casares on the Costa del Sol (right). Below: Resort town on the Costa Blanca*

# GREEN SPAIN

Many of the cities and towns discussed thus far are in regions of the country that are hot most of the year and have very little rainfall. But there is another region called Costa Verde ("the green coast"), along the north and northwestern reaches of the nation, bordering on the Atlantic Ocean. "Green Spain," as it is also known, has rainfall on an average of 125 days a year, compared with only about 15 days in the semiarid southeast. As a result, the landscape resembles southern Ireland, with its lush, green vegetation and small lakes and streams.

This northern region of Spain includes three ancient historic regions—Galicia, Asturias, and the Basque country—and the maritime province of Santander. The most important cities here are San Sebastián, Bilbao, Santander, La Coruña, and Pontevedra.

San Sebastián is in the Basque region, near the southwestern border of France. It huddles on the Bay of Biscay at the mouth of the Urumea River. Its site is picturesque, with Mount Urgull rising as a backdrop inland. The present city is relatively new, having been rebuilt largely during the nineteenth century. Much of San Sebastián had been destroyed in the Peninsular War during a vicious battle between the British, under the Duke of Wellington, and the French troops of Napoleon in 1813.

Many stately homes have been built along this part of the coast, particularly near the village of Fuenterrabía on the outskirts of San Sebastián. The area is one of the most fashionable seaside resorts for Spaniards and is also a summer residence of royalty. Its fame really developed in the late nineteenth century, when ocean bathing and seaside strolling first became "acceptable" and wealthy Spaniards began to desert the large cities for small seaside

*Bilbao*

resorts during the hot months. San Sebastián continues to be popular for its beaches, hotels, and outstanding restaurants.

A little more than fifty miles (eighty kilometers) west of San Sebastián is Bilbao, a city of more than 400,000 people. Bilbao straddles both banks of the Nervión River. After its founding in the fourteenth century on the site of an ancient and little-known civilization, it flourished as a wool-export center for three hundred years. Its commercial fortunes declined steadily until the nineteenth century, when its citizens began developing heavy industry. Today it again flourishes as one of the Atlantic's leading ports, known for shipbuilding and the production of chemicals and steel.

Bilbao is possibly the most "English" of all major Spanish cities because of the part the British played in developing its industry. Bilbao's real economic growth started when the British began developing nearby iron mines during the second half of the nineteenth century.

*Santander is noted for its beaches and monuments.*

Outside this industrial city—and not far away—the landscape goes back to nature. The winding coastal roads run through beautiful countryside and mountainous terrain, blanketed with lush green forests. In contrast to the subtropical regions that make up the southern coasts of Spain, this environment is temperate, with cool autumns and cold winters.

Driving west for two hours takes the traveler to Santander, which is both a seaport and a popular summer resort. Like Bilbao, the city's industry is strongly based on the nearby iron mines. Like San Sebastián, the land along the coast is the site of fine summer mansions, including a former royal summer palace. Many buildings in the heart of Santander are new, replacing the thirteenth-century cathedral and the business district that were destroyed by fire in 1941.

Santander, the port of Old Castile, is the center of a cluster of fashionable summer resorts that are active during the warm months but quiet at other seasons.

*Cable cars
take skiers
and sightseers
up the
Picos de Europa.*

The whole province of Santander is noted for its dairy cattle. Not far from the city are vast pasturelands, green meadows, and narrow, tree-lined highways with verdant hedgerows. Inland, to the southwest of the city, the magnificent mountains of the Picos de Europa ("Peaks of Europe") stand out against the sky, heightening the rich greenness of the countryside. Trout fishing is a favorite pastime here. Mountain streams plunge into deep gorges and the air is fresh with the scent of balsam and pine.

Mountain climbing and skiing are popular, too. The region offers views comparable to those in Switzerland. This is the region, too, of rugged rock formations and endless caves, including the famous Altamira caves with their Paleolithic wall paintings. Several museums at Altamira and Santander exhibit utensils, ornaments, and weapons from these caves that are ten thousand to twenty thousand years old. As the home of cavemen and other primitive tribes, this part of Spain can well claim to be one of the oldest in the country—and even in all of Europe.

*La Coruña harbor*

These mountain regions west of Santander were strongholds for Visigoth warriors retreating in the eighth century from the Moors. What started as a matter of survival in this region, called Asturias, eventually became the crusade that overpowered the Moors and forced them back to North Africa. According to legend, it was Pelayo, a king of Oviedo, who first rallied the people in these mountains for the resistance movement.

The northwestern tip of Spain, at what is known as the *cornisa* ("cornice") of the Atlantic, is the site of La Coruña. Situated some 450 miles (724 kilometers) west of the French border, where the Bay of Biscay ends, La Coruña is often wild and stormy. The winter season brings northerly gales, during which local vessels make quick runs for La Coruña's harbor, which is a busy commercial port year-round.

La Coruña reached its peak as a port and an important textile center in the late Middle Ages. It was from here, for example, that the Spanish Armada sailed in 1588, heading due north to the

*Replica of Columbus's* Santa María *in Barcelona's harbor*

English Channel. Here, too, the city was invaded from the sea and sacked ten years later by Sir Francis Drake, and a bloody battle was fought during the Peninsular War. The city today has an important fishing industry, as well as shipyards and metalworks.

Finally, on the northern coastal strip along the Atlantic, is Pontevedra. Like La Coruña, it is part of the Galicia region of Spain. Pontevedra is a fishing port at the mouth of the Lérez River, as well as a manufacturing center for leather goods, clothing, fertilizers, and farm implements. It is said that Christopher Columbus was born here, although the facts are not clear. It is certain, though, that at least one of his ships, the *Santa María,* was built in the town's shipyard.

One of the significant features of Pontevedra is that it lies so close to the border of Spain's neighbor, Portugal. Many navigators and seamen, like Columbus, learned their trade in Portugal and sailed on Portuguese ships.

Two examples of Spain's expanding industrialization: a quarry in
Buelles (above) and an electronics technician in Rota (below)

# Chapter 5

# A LAND OF SURPRISES

---

As recently as the 1960s, Spain's economy was based heavily on agriculture. But by the early 1980s, Spain was listed tenth among the world's industrial nations. How did this transformation come about?

Spain has always been a land of surprises. Its geography and climate are so diverse that it has been called a "miniature continent." Its people, too, reflect a wealth of cultural and ethnic backgrounds and have pursued a wide range of trades and callings for many generations. As a crossroad of migrating peoples from Europe, Africa, and the Americas for centuries, Spain has become a land where transitions are commonplace. Thus, it has been relatively easy for Spain to make the change from an agrarian to an industrial economy.

An increase in foreign trade in the early 1960s also stimulated industrial development. Trade with other countries became less restricted, partly because of an increase in tourism. This brought more money into the country and made it possible to purchase more imports. Another factor was the influx of workers into the industrial centers, as more and more people moved from farms

*Wheat is one of Spain's most important crops.*

and rural areas to the cities. A third important development was that foreign banks began increasing their investments in Spain as they saw that the nation was on the verge of developing its industries.

## AGRICULTURAL BACKGROUND

Before Spain became industrialized, the nation's economy was built on agriculture for many hundreds of years. Until the end of the 1950s, Spain was engaged in what is known as "traditional" agriculture. The land was composed mainly of large estates and small farms. Since there was an overabundance of workers, wages were very low and farm products were low priced.

Spain's most important crops are wheat, barley, and corn; garden vegetables, such as potatoes, tomatoes, and onions; and fruits and nuts, such as oranges, apples, mandarins, and almonds. The production of grapes has been increasing as Spain's wines have achieved world renown.

*Grape production is growing to meet the demand for Spanish wines.*

But many other crops are in serious decline. Wheat and barley were falling off badly by the middle of the 1980s. Sheep farmers were facing a declining market. And almonds were less and less in demand as other countries lowered their almond prices. In just two decades, during the 1960s and 1970s, the value of agriculture in Spain dropped from 22.6 percent to 8.1 percent of the gross national product (the total value of everything produced within a country).

During the 1980s, agriculture showed signs of strengthening (as in the case of vineyards), though only in certain regions. One of the major problems has always been the shortage of water and the immense variations in rainfall. Climate plays a vital role, both positive and negative, in the harvest.

One region whose agriculture is always highly profitable is the east coast along the Mediterranean Sea. There, the combination of warm climate, sunny days, and adequate moisture is ideal for cultivating fruits and vegetables.

Cork tree

## FOREST PRESERVATION

Most of the natural forests on the Iberian Peninsula disappeared long ago. Changes in climate and rainfall, erosion, and insect pests brought about severe losses. But much of the blame goes to generations of inhabitants who stripped the forests for firewood, buildings, or farmland.

Not until the end of the 1930s did Spain undertake a major reforestation program. One goal has been to control natural erosion and insect pests. Another has been to plant new trees, especially poplar, eucalyptus, and a variety of pines and other evergreens that grow fast.

The cork oak is one of Spain's most important trees because it can grow in arid climates and in poor soils. Spain is second only to Portugal in producing cork.

The preservation of cork trees is very important because a tree may have to grow fifty years before it can produce as much as 100 pounds (45 kilograms) of good-quality cork during one stripping.

*Shipbuilding (left). Barcelona's Naval Museum (right)*

Cork, which is actually the bark of the tree, can be stripped from each tree only once every ten years. Even then, it must be removed very carefully so as not to damage future crops. A tree can yield as much as 500 pounds (227 kilograms) of cork by the time it reaches the age of eighty. The best-quality cork, grown in the Catalonia region, is used for bottle corks.

## INDUSTRIAL EXPANSION

"Spain's rapid industrial development in the 1960s and early 1970s resulted in one of Western Europe's most impressive growth rates." So read a report on European industries and economies. According to the study, the areas of greatest growth were manufacturing and the production of gas and electricity.

Spain is one of the top five shipbuilding countries in the world. It has more than forty shipyards capable of building steel-hulled vessels ranging from fishing boats to huge supertankers.

Except for coal, which had become scarce after many generations of mining, the country had few energy resources other than the forests, which also were seriously depleted. There are two minor sources of petroleum: an offshore oil deposit in the northwestern Mediterranean near Tarragona and an onshore field near Burgos in the north. Spain thus has to import more than 60 percent of its petroleum. Despite its domestic coal reserves, Spain also has to import a great deal of coal for steelmaking.

As recently as the late nineteenth century, Spain was Europe's leading producer of copper, mercury, lead, and iron ore. But by the middle of the twentieth century, the only minerals of world significance were mercury and sulfur. These are still produced in small quantities, along with manganese, tin, uranium, and zinc.

## TOURISM, THE GREAT NEW "COMMODITY"

According to the Spain-U.S. Chamber of Commerce, the "most-visited site in Spain" is not the world-renowned Prado Museum of Art or the Royal Palace in Madrid, but the Alhambra. Situated in the southern city of Granada, this Moorish palace attracts over 1.5 million visitors each year.

Remarkably, this group of ancient buildings, constructed between 1230 and 1354, lay almost in ruins a century and a half ago. Earmarked for destruction, they were saved and restored largely because of a famous American author, Washington Irving. While serving as an attaché at the American embassy in Madrid, he became fascinated by the ruined palace and, in 1832, wrote *Tales of the Alhambra*, a book that soon became popular in Europe and America alike. Partly as a result of his book, the Alhambra was restored for posterity.

This palace is just one of the thousands of reasons that Spain attracts forty million foreign visitors a year, a figure equal to its own population. Many come to visit the historic sites and ancient buildings, to absorb the deep-rooted culture of Spain, to study the art, or to enjoy the towns and villages that have changed very little over many generations.

But the tourist boom really began in the mid-1950s when European vacationers began discovering the beaches, the sunny shores, and the warm climate of Spain's Mediterranean seacoasts. Word spread quickly. From fewer than one million tourists in

1950, the figure climbed to thirty-five million in a little over two decades and kept on rising. By the beginning of the 1980s, tourism was bringing in $7 billion a year.

Someone once determined that the total number of visitors from Portugal over a one-year period equaled half the population of Portugal, while the number from France equaled one-fourth of that country's population. Spaniards themselves are important tourists in their own country. They flock in huge numbers to the beaches and seaside towns, both on the Mediterranean and on the Atlantic. They are attracted by the sights and events of Madrid and Seville and other large cities. And they travel from all corners of the nation to the sites of annual fiestas and fairs.

Tourism brings its problems—such as overcrowding, extreme variations in population, and the rapid construction of cheaply-built hotels and restaurants. But it greatly strengthens the Spanish economy. Tourists bring in dollars and other currency from abroad, just as exports do. During the years when tourism drops off, people invariably notice empty apartments and half-occupied hotels and talk of "overbuilding." Yet the boom years were responsible for improvements in the highways, the airports, and other systems of transportation and communication.

One such example was the creation of the *Transcantábrico*, a luxury train service designed to rival any on the continent. The longest narrow-gauge railway in Europe, it runs some 625 miles (1,006 kilometers) across the superb mountain ranges of Cantabria, covering almost the entire coastline of northern Spain. Creating this tourist attraction required the meticulous renovation of antique passenger coaches and sleeping cars. Its locomotives had to be capable of navigating the tight curves and steep inclines of the peaks and valleys along its route.

*Granada's Parador San Francisco was once a medieval monastery.*

During the last half-century, Spain has developed a unique type
of tourist facility that greatly appeals to foreign visitors. This is the
*parador* ("hostelry" or "inn"), of which there are almost a
hundred all across the countryside. Variously described as
"wayside inns," "mountain shelters," and "refuges," many of
them are ancient or historical buildings that have been restored.
They may once have been castles, monasteries, convents,
fortresses, or even palaces. The parador in Úbeda, for example,
was built as a palace in the sixteenth century; the one at Carmona
blends with a walled Moorish fortress; while another, at
Guadalupe, was a shelter built in the fifteenth century for pilgrims
visiting a nearby shrine. The paradors were meant to attract
travelers not only to the traditional tourist sites, but also to
outlying areas that previously had poor accommodations. As a
result, the paradors have come to be known as some of the most
reliable inns in all of Europe, making it possible to tour the
remotest areas of the country in comfort.

Mountain tunnels have been cut through the Catalonian Pyrenees
(above). Fresh seafood (below) is abundant in Spain.

Spain's roads and other transportation systems radiate from Madrid, in the center of the nation. Driving to outlying towns and villages can be difficult and slow, except in major tourist areas.

Railroads cover less than 15,000 miles (24,135 kilometers). In many regions, service is provided to only major cities and resorts. Train service can be slow, particularly in the mountainous regions of the north, where the tracks wind around tangles of mountain peaks and through tunnels. Sharp curves, trestles, and steep inclines make train travel picturesque, if not very fast.

Air transportation has improved greatly since the middle of the 1960s. Spain has about twenty major airports near major cities, and an equal number of second-class airports in other locations. Iberia is the national airline.

## FISHING AND FISHERIES

Fishing has been the livelihood of seacoast people of the Iberian Peninsula since prehistoric times. Artifacts found in caves along the northeastern coast reveal that primitive tribes caught fish from the waters of the nearby Atlantic, or at least from sea inlets. Thousands of years later, the seagoing people who reached the peninsula by crossing the Mediterranean found their most reliable source of food in the new land to be fish. Consequently, many of the ships they built were designed specifically for fishing, often far out at sea.

Spain ranks among the top five or six fishing nations in the world. It is well known for its sardines and anchovies, as well as tuna, hake, and cod, most of which come from the Atlantic. The Canary Islands are noted for their excellent lobsters and other shellfish, and are popular for deep-sea sports fishing.

*Art has flourished in Spain for centuries: a prehistoric Altamira cave painting (above); Pablo Picasso artwork in a Barcelona office building (below)*

# Chapter 6

# *CULTURE THROUGH MANY AGES*

Few countries can claim that the foundations for their art were laid twenty thousand years ago. Yet such is the case with Spain, where the earliest artistic expressions are the paintings rendered by Stone Age hunters on the walls of the famous caves at Altamira. Sketched in black and red, probably by the light of primitive log fires, their purpose may have been to work some kind of magic to ensure success in the next day's hunt. Other cave paintings are more abstract than the realistic boars, deer, horses, and bison that can be seen today at Altamira. These are considered one of the earliest forms of communication, comparable to the hieroglyphics of the ancient Egyptians.

From these unique beginnings, Spanish art blossomed into a montage of many types and forms, as it was successively influenced by the many peoples who passed through this "crossroads" of western Europe. Some of the art influenced the entire Iberian Peninsula. Much of it, though, was regional, developing in areas where the outsiders' influence was strongest.

Aside from prehistoric works, the country's true artistic heritage began with the works of the Celts and Iberians. These early inhabitants created imaginative scenes on vases and bowls. Some common subjects were battle scenes and feats of horsemanship.

*The* Dama de Elche,
*an Iberian sculpture*

Examples of Iberian art are rare. Most are in the form of clay statues. One of the most famous is called *Dama de Elche* (Lady of Elche). It dates from the fifth century B.C. and was probably influenced by the Greeks.

## THE ROMAN INFLUENCE

The Roman occupation, from the third century B.C. to the fifth century A.D., heralded a period when art and architecture began to flourish. One of the major contributions of the Romans was a diversity of materials. Besides clay and ceramics, they used gold, silver, copper, iron, and lead for statues and jewelry.

Art and architecture were skillfully blended, and many examples have been found and preserved throughout Spain. The Romans used their engineering skills to construct roads, strong bridges, elegant public baths, long aqueducts, beautiful amphitheaters, and resplendent fountains. At the same time, they

*Roman mosaic*

decorated these public works with colorful mosaics, bas-reliefs, statues, and inlays of precious metals. Because they used materials that endured, many Roman masterpieces still exist. Even the roads used for commerce and troop movements were embellished here and there with mosaics and marked by roadside monuments.

Except for Italy, no other Western nation has preserved so many monuments from this epoch in history. After twenty centuries, many Roman bridges and aqueducts in Spain are still being used. Notable examples are the aqueduct at Segovia, which dates from the first century A.D., a bridge over the river Tagus, the Proserpina dike in Badajoz, and the "Tower of Hercules" that forms the lighthouse at La Coruña.

The Visigoths, who replaced the Romans in the sixth and seventh centuries, left no painting or sculpture and surprisingly little architecture. However, they were known for their artistry in creating jewelry inlaid with gold, bas-relief coins, decorative crosses, and religious ornaments.

*A typical Islamic geometrical design at the Alhambra*

## ARRIVAL OF THE MOORS

At the beginning of the eighth century, the invading Moors brought with them far more than weapons of war. They introduced new art forms and figures thought of today as being typically "Spanish." The dominant medium for Arabic artistic expression was architecture. The horseshoe arch, more than any other single object, symbolized Moorish design.

In their mosques and palaces, the Moors perfected techniques that persist today in Spanish design. One was the skill with which they "framed" their interiors through the location of archways. Another was an ingenious way of achieving natural lighting effects and offsetting them with areas of shade and shadow. A third Arab "trademark" that found its way into Spanish design was the repetition of motifs to form a harmonious whole.

The Moors also influenced the design of Christian churches, not only throughout Spain but elsewhere in Europe. One of the most impressive Moslem buildings is the mosque built at Córdoba in the late eighth century. Other outstanding examples are in two cities that were major Arabic centers: Toledo and Zaragoza. In the twelfth century, Seville was the setting for the construction of the Giralda Tower, noted for its arched windows.

The greatest masterpiece of Moorish architecture in Spain is the Alhambra palace at Granada, the seat of Moslem rulers from the thirteenth century until the city was captured by King Ferdinand and Queen Isabella in 1492.

## CULTURAL TRENDS IN NORTHERN SPAIN

Shortly before the Moors were expelled from Spain, the influence of the French was beginning to be felt in the north. This led to the introduction of the Romanesque style of architecture. Much simpler in design and less ornate than earlier forms of architecture, it is characterized by its solidarity and strength and the use of rounded, rather than horseshoe, arches.

Another style, which lasted from the twelfth to the eighteenth century, was *Mudéjar*, sometimes referred to as "the most genuine of the Spanish artistic styles." It was developed in the Christian centers of Spain, but combined Moorish techniques and designs. Mudéjar is characterized by the use of bricks and plaster and ceilings that are richly decorated, following the Arab custom. Much of this art was lost over the centuries because of the perishable nature of the materials, such as ceramics and stucco. Two of the most vivid examples of Mudéjar style are El Salvador Tower in Teruel and Coca Castle in Segovia.

*The Hispano-Flemish Church of San Juan de los Reyes in Toledo*

The Gothic influence also filtered down from France, but showed Flemish and German influences as well. It lasted until the seventeenth century and was a characteristic mark of the Middle Ages. The interiors of Gothic churches were elaborately sculptured, while paintings abounded everywhere—on the walls and ceilings as well as on choir stalls, altars, pews, and tombs.

Later, the Gothic style was to have a Spanish counterpart, known as Hispano-Flemish. It was highly decorative and became popular in the construction of churches and monasteries as well as public buildings. The most influential building in this style was probably the Church of San Juan de los Reyes in Toledo.

## THE GOLDEN AGE

In the sixteenth century Spanish art and architecture blossomed into the period known as the Spanish Renaissance. Many great masters contributed to the development of art in this period.

*El Greco's* Adoration of the Shepherds *features the elongated, mystical figures that are his trademark.*

One of the great painters of the Renaissance was Domenikos Theotokopoulous. As his name implies, he was not Spanish at all, but Greek. Today he is better known as El Greco ("The Greek"). Although El Greco was born on the island of Crete in 1541 and was a student of the great master Titian in Italy, he became associated with Spain after moving to Toledo to paint the altar of the Church of Santo Domingo. Deeply religious, he imbued his paintings with a mystical quality that has amazed his admirers for centuries. His figures are strangely elongated, with silvery highlights that seem to mesmerize the viewer.

The Baroque period followed the Renaissance. Baroque religious subjects were more emotional in tone and sometimes starkly realistic. Francisco de Zurbarán was one of the outstanding painters of this period. He was a contemporary of Velázquez, one of the greatest figures in the history of art. Velázquez was a close

*Francisco Goya's* Execution of May 3, 1808

friend of King Philip IV, a patron of the arts. Other Spanish artists of the seventeenth and eighteenth centuries whose works are popular today are Murillo and Goya.

## MODERN ART

Spanish painting declined at the end of the 1600s and through much of the 1700s before it was revived by Francisco Goya. Goya painted portraits with great realism. He sometimes angered his subjects by highlighting blemishes and disfigurements that they preferred to have ignored. He was noted for his imaginative, and sometimes frightening, depictions of bullfighters or soldiers in action. He was able to use quick, simple strokes with great effect.

After Goya died in 1828, only a few painters in Spain had the stature of masters until the twentieth century. The greatest figure in modern Spanish art was to be Pablo Picasso (1881-1973). Born

*Sidewalk artist in Barcelona (left). The central salon
of the Prado Museum of Art in Madrid (right)*

a Spaniard, he left Spain to settle in Paris when he was twenty-
three and was associated with French art until his death at the age
of ninety-two. In his adopted country, he was honored by being
the only artist ever to have his work hung in the Louvre art
museum during his lifetime. However, Picasso was always
acclaimed by Spaniards who were proud of his achievements.

Other modern Spanish artists of note are Juan Gris, who
worked with Picasso in Paris; José Gutiérrez Solana, who depicted
the poor; Joan Miró, a Catalonian whose paintings are colorful
and abstract; and Salvador Dalí, who achieved great popularity
(as well as criticism) for surrealist paintings that range from the
humorous to the outrageous.

Much of the best and most representative work of Spanish
artists down through history can be seen at the Prado Museum in
Madrid, which contains one of the most famous art collections in
the world. Located in the heart of the city, it is a formidable
eighteenth-century building surrounded by parks and gardens.

91

# THE LITERATURE OF SPAIN

Spanish literature originated long before there was even a Spanish language. For almost a thousand years, literary figures in Spain were Roman and wrote in Latin. Noted among them were Seneca, Lucan, Martial, and Quintilian. As late as the tenth and eleventh centuries, many of the outstanding writings—mostly religious works or poetry—were written in the native tongues of Moslems and Jews who lived in the southern and central regions of the country. The first major work in Spanish was *Poema de Mío Cid* (*Poem of the Cid*), written in the early thirteenth century. Its subject was a national hero known as the Cid Campeador. The epic poem describes his adventures and how he saved the old city of Valencia from the invading Arabs. During that same century, the romantic Spanish lyric appeared. One of the most noted was entitled "The Reason of Love."

Although all of these early works were written in a form of Spanish, many were in regional dialects that bore little resemblance to the modern-day language. During the next two or three centuries, many of the most famous Oriental works of the era were translated into Castilian, which was emerging as the purest form of the Spanish language. The fourteenth century ushered in a number of books of parables and tales, most of which presented some kind of moral, rather than simply telling a story.

It was commonplace to borrow legends and epics from the literature of other countries. Arabic stories were popular. So were the legends of King Arthur, Charlemagne, and the classical Greek and Roman heroes. The first Spanish novel was *El Caballero Cifar* (*The Knight Cifar*), which dramatized the events of a knight and his lady-love.

*Miguel de Cervantes's characters, the adventuresome Don Quixote and his faithful squire Sancho Panza, are known and loved throughout the world.*

Many of these works were written in longhand and read to small groups of listeners. Some, like the lyric poems, were sung as ballads. And many were simply told from memory. It was not until 1474 that printing was introduced in Spain, making it possible to publish books. Even then, few were printed.

As with architecture and art, the last half of the sixteenth century and most of the seventeenth century formed literature's Golden Age. It started with the publication of works of two of the period's greatest poets, Juan Boscán Almogáver and Garcilaso de la Vega. By far the best-known book of this period was the novel *Don Quixote de la Mancha* by Miguel de Cervantes. One of the masterpieces of world literature, its publication stirred great interest in the romantic novel, and it had many imitators.

*Lope de Vega Carpio*

The Golden Age also saw the development of early Spanish drama. One of the major playwrights—and one of the most prolific authors in history—was Lope de Vega Carpio, who wrote tragedies, comedies, and religious plays. A friend of Cervantes, he was responsible for founding the theater in Spain. He is said to have written almost two thousand plays, more than five hundred of which survive today. Calderón de la Barca, who wrote during the seventeenth century, was the best dramatist of this era, however, and was well known outside of Spain also.

Following the Golden Age there were very few writers of note for a period of more than a century. This was partly because of political problems and partly because royalty was more interested in French culture.

When Ferdinand VII died in 1833, Spain was suddenly swept by a torrent of romanticism, largely based on the romantic movement that was current in England and France. The trend was a reaction to the deteriorating political situation and to the problems that were keeping Spain from attaining stature in Europe. Among the

*Luis de Góngora*

best writers of this period are Zorrilla, Espronceda, Larra, Campoamor, and Becquer. There followed a group of novelists known as the "naturalists," including Pereda, Pérez Galdós, and Emilia Pardo Bazán.

At the beginning of the twentieth century, the literature of the country was deeply—and adversely—affected by the nation's losses in the Spanish-American War and the decline of Spain's colonial empire. One positive reaction, however, was the birth of a new movement known as *modernismo* ("modernism"). It was stimulated by a group of poets who had been inspired by one of the greatest poets of the Golden Age, Luis de Góngora. Once again, lyric poetry flourished in Spain, led by the two most influential members of the *modernismo* movement, Rubén Darío (born in Nicaragua) and Juan Ramón Jiménez.

During the 1930s and 1940s, many of Spain's best writers lived outside the country. Like Picasso, they could not tolerate the political atmosphere that pervaded Spain. Nor could they subject themselves to the censorship and restrictions that plagued writers under the Franco regime. The writings of García Lorca, Manuel Machado, and Miguel Hernández were banned.

The most renowned Spanish author of modern times is Federico García Lorca. He was known for his poetry, versatility, and imaginative plays. He died tragically, shot while he was in prison in 1936 during the Spanish civil war.

## EDUCATION

Spanish education was greatly enriched by the many cultures that blended during the nation's formation. Education made great strides during the long period of Roman rule. Yet it was limited almost exclusively to the upper classes. A number of universities were founded during the fourteenth and fifteenth centuries. The University of Salamanca, the oldest in Spain, can be traced back to the twelfth century.

Many of the universities and schools went into a period of decline during the Middle Ages. At best, they were weakened by poor teaching and superstition. After getting off to a good start historically, education fell far behind that of most of the major European nations. The Roman Catholic church played a dominant role in Spanish education, from the Middle Ages to about the middle of the twentieth century. For all but the ruling class, the only schools available were those established by the church.

It was not until the middle of the nineteenth century that the Spanish government instituted public schools. These schools, however, were mainly in the cities and gave little opportunity to young people who lived in small towns and rural districts. Today there are schools at all levels throughout Spain, providing education for rich and poor alike.

*The Catholic University of Comillas (above)*
*University students in Salamanca (below)*

*Above: Sorting seaweed (left). Doorstep merchants in Mallorca (right)*
*Below: Seasoned citizen of Barcelona (left). Children of Córdoba (right)*

# Chapter 7

# A LAND WITH
## MANY FACES

There is an old saying that "Spain is not one nation but a multitude."

This can be seen in Spain's history, with the influence of the many peoples who crossed over its borders. It is seen in the country's diversity of regions and provinces, many with basic language differences. And the saying surely rings true when considering the range of life-styles found in Spain, not only from east to west and north to south, but within any given district.

Spaniards in general are a proud people, regardless of economic status or social position. This pride is reflected, sometimes fiercely, in devotion to their communities. It tends to grow weaker as it extends outward to the province and then to the nation. Nevertheless, a Catalonian from the northeast is likely to defend the virtues of his province very stoutly to an Andalusian from the southwest—and vice versa.

*Statue of the Roman philosopher Seneca in Córdoba*

The Roman writer and philosopher Seneca, who was born in Córdoba, advised his Spanish neighbors, "Do not let yourself be conquered by anything alien to your spirit." He was well aware of the pride and determination of the citizens of the land that Roman troops had invaded. The stoicism he envisioned has characterized the people down through the ages.

## DOING IT THEIR OWN WAY

Generalizations about the nature of people are risky to make. Yet it does seem that throughout Spain people do tend to be individualistic. They will complete whatever tasks are necessary, but only in their own time and in their own way. The most universal evidence of this is the siesta, a two- or three-hour break during the day, when working people either return to their homes or enjoy long, relaxed lunch hours. The custom has persisted to the present day (although in Madrid and other large cities this is

*Enjoying a chess game at siesta time in Madrid*

beginning to change). Banks close, stores shut their doors, transportation dwindles, government offices become empty, and practically everyone forgets the hustle and bustle.

An American journalist, covering Spain during the height of the tragic Spanish civil war, once reported with astonishment that "military advances stopped temporarily, guns were silenced, and fighter planes flew back to their bases" each day at noon. Since the adversaries on both sides were Spaniards, they saw nothing unusual about taking a siesta, even at a time of battle.

## FOOD AND WINE

Lunch is only one of the Spaniards' two main meals. Dinner, served around 9 P.M. or even later, is the second one. Although Spanish cooking does not have the reputation that French cuisine does, there is a rich variety of regional dishes, some of them renowned around the world. *Paella,* a dish from Valencia made

*A dish of* paella *(left). Wine cellar in Jerez de la Frontera (right)*

with chicken, seafoods, and rice, is cooked on an open fire of grapevines and olive branches. It is colored and spiced with saffron, which gives it a bright yellow coloring, and cooked and served in a special pan, or *paellera. Gazpacho,* a cold soup made of green peppers, cucumbers, and tomatoes with a dash of olive oil, vinegar, and ground cumin seeds, is a trademark of Andalusia, but is served everywhere on hot summer days.

Spain is a land of vineyards, and each region produces its own wines. The most famous are the red wines of Rioja, produced along the banks of the Ebro, and the Jerez or sherry wines of Jerez de la Frontera in southwestern Andalusia. Dry or sweet sherry is poured into a long, narrow glass and enjoyed before dinner.

## ARTS AND CRAFTS

Spain, isolated at the southern tip of Europe, has kept native craftsmanship very much alive. Each region has a distinctive type

*Ceramics (left), inlaid damascene steel (center), and a partially-woven tapestry (right)*

of ceramics that reflects its heritage. In Andalusia, geometric designs continue the tradition of Islam, the religion of the Moors, which prohibited making pictures of living things. In Castile, designs of birds and game in blue and yellow recall the life of kings and peasants.

History is present in every form of craft, but the damascene steel of Toledo and the leather of Córdoba take us back to the Moors and their splendor. In Toledo, where the finest swords are made, artisans still inlay steel with gold and silver threads, following a centuries-old tradition. They use a stylet and a small hammer to create beautiful designs for swords, jewelry, plates, boxes, ashtrays, and various other objects.

Steel and leather crafts are generally handled by men, but women are the artists who meticulously and patiently make Spanish laces and embroideries for tablecloths and clothing. Each region has its own special designs and color of threads. The art of tapestry weaving is another fine native craft.

*Flamenco dancers performing in Seville*

## THE SOUL OF SPAIN

Guitars and castanets are the essence of Spanish popular music. Although each province has its own folk dances and music, flamenco in Andalusia, based on popular folklore, has reached a high artistic level. The flamenco song or *cante jondo* is of Oriental origin, and is best sung by the Spanish Gypsies or *gitanos*. Based on modulations of a single vowel or syllable, flamenco songs resemble a lament. The best singers are known only by their nickname or their birthplace.

Flamenco dance is characterized by the expression of the hands, the movement of the chest, and the footwork or *zapateado*, a type of tapdancing. It is said that, to be good, the dancer has to be possessed by the demon of inspiration, or *duende*.

Flamenco songs and dances are improvisations and involve audience response, much as in American blues music. Twentieth-century classical musicians, such as Manuel de Falla,

*Semana Santa in Seville (left); the Fiesta la Patum in Barcelona (right)*

Isaac Albéniz, and Enrique Granados, have incorporated flamenco music into their compositions.

## FIESTA TIME

Many of the holidays in Spain are religious feasts and are celebrated in the streets. The best known is Holy Week or Semana Santa, which begins on Palm Sunday and ends on Easter Saturday. Every day, processions of floats supporting richly attired and bejeweled religious statues pass through the streets, followed by penitents in long robes and high pointed hoods that cover their faces. In Castile these ceremonies express a tragic feeling, but in Andalusia they are colorful representations of Christ's passion. The processions take place at sundown, accompanied by the rhythm of special march music and lighted by torches. Suddenly, from the crowd, arises a piercing, short song or *saeta*, expressing sorrow, pain, or ecstasy.

*Bullfights (left) and soccer (right) compete for favorite sport.*

Another popular fiesta which takes place from mid-March until October is the bullfight, or *corrida*. As precisely calculated as a ballet, the *corrida* is a colorful spectacle representing the combat of man against beast, of intelligence against brute strength. The *corrida* has several acts, like a play. It culminates with the death of the bull, although the outcome is never certain—many a bullfighter has died in the arena, such as Manolete, who is still considered the greatest bullfighter of all time.

Related to the bullfight, the festivities of San Fermín in the northern town of Pamplona involve the whole population. A herd of bulls is let loose at the entrance to the city as many of the braver townspeople run ahead of them. Through the narrow streets, from balconies and doorsteps, onlookers encourage men and beasts on their way to the arena.

Although a sport, soccer could be considered a ritual. From the time they can barely walk, boys exercise their skill with a soccer ball. On fields, street corners, squares, and public gardens, they try

Tapas *are a favorite snack for young and old alike.*

their best at making goals. As for baseball and football, the American and European championships are followed eagerly.

## MEETING FRIENDS

Spaniards love children, and Spanish families are often quite large. Although many activities, such as daily meals, involve the whole family, youngsters are fairly free.

Apart from soccer, meeting friends and sharing activities with them is an important pastime for Spanish youngsters. On evenings and weekends, boys and girls converge on the town plaza or main square gathering in groups called *pandillas*. As they grow into young adulthood they still meet, chatting and laughing as they walk around the square until dinnertime.

Once in a while they may go *de tascas*. A *tasca* is a bar that opens onto the street and serves a variety of little snacks called *tapas*, A lot of *tapas* can be the equivalent of a full meal.

# REGIONAL PERSONALITIES

A knowledgeable observer of Spaniards can guess where they are from by their speech, style of dress, mannerisms, and other telltale factors. There are marked differences from one region or province to another. The following are examples.

*Galicians.* The people here in the northwestern tip of Spain reflect the nature of their environment. It is a land of rugged mountains where many of the homes are solidly built of stone and where many of the facilities are primitive. There is something of Scotland in the nature of the people as well as the land. They have a dour, melancholy outlook and are at the same time deeply sentimental about their communities, their families, and their heritage. Many Galicians have such a passionate love of their homeland that they become sick if circumstances force them to move to another country or province. This illness — homesickness, actually — is so real that it has a name — *morriña* ("sadness" or "melancholia") — and has been the subject of many songs and ballads.

Galicia has been home for myriads of writers and singers, going back to the days of the minstrels in the thirteenth century. Many of the stories and ballads take their themes from the nature of the environment. They depict the plaintive nostalgia of men forced to leave Galicia to go off to battle, or of mysterious spirits that haunt the forests and mountains. The Galicians, like their Celtic counterparts in Scotland and Ireland, also play the bagpipes.

Galicians are always in love with their land, with the lush valleys, the pine-clad hills, the torrential streams. For them, it is the heart of Spain and all else is foreign.

*Basques.* On both sides of the Pyrenees Mountains live the

*Bagpipers on their way to a festival in La Coruña (left). Many Basques still wear the characteristic beret, or* boina *(right).*

Basques, a people whose origins are obscure. They call their country Euskadi and speak Euskara, or Basque. The Basque language was spoken before the Romans conquered Spain, and experts differ regarding its origin.

A seafaring people made even more rugged by the mountainous terrain they inhabit, the Basques are physically strong. They enjoy the reputation of eating a lot and of playing exhausting games like *pelota*, a game similar to squash, and *passolaris*, a weight-lifting game.

Basques are proud of their race, very independent, and obstinate. They are good seamen, renowned as whale fishermen, and excellent shepherds. Their strength and high spirits have made them good soldiers, and they took an active part in the colonization of the Americas, being the founders of Buenos Aires, Argentina.

The Basque language became an official local language in 1978 and is actively revived in education and literature. A segment of the Basque population would like to see their region become a separate nation.

*Catalans.* Living on the northeastern tip of Spain, the natives of Catalonia approach life in a practical way. Many of them, particularly in the great city of Barcelona, are business-minded, and not a few are entrepreneurs who have started their own small ventures. They tend to be industrious and thrifty, with great respect for the *peseta.* Catalan society is more open than the Basque society to its west, possibly because its people are accustomed to dealing with strangers. The people are communicative, having a strong literary tradition that was influenced by French troubadours six centuries ago.

Catalans are among the most practical minded in all of Spain. They have to be, since they have elected to develop their region into one of the most important industrial areas in the country. Yet they tenaciously cling to historical traditions, notably to the Catalan language itself, which in the past often was banned in schools and official businesses.

*Castilians.* The character of the Castilians has long been honed by the nature of the land they occupy, in the arid central region of Spain. "The Castilians are a dry and frugal breed," wrote an American author who had come to know these people over many years, "inured alike to sun and cold, sinewy of body, and with the stern dignity of dethroned kings." The reference to royalty stems from the fact that the vast plateau occupied by Castile once was composed of the ancient kingdoms of León, Old Castile, New Castile, and La Mancha. Over the years, Castilian became the most widely recognized mother tongue, in provincial Spain and the colonies alike. Today it is a basic language for more than 250 million people around the world.

The people of Castile dwell—as they always have—in towns
and villages separated by many miles of desolate plains. Hence,
they sometimes tend to be closed to outsiders. They inherited a
fear of strangers when, hundreds of years ago, their ancestors
were constantly under attack by Moors and other invaders.
Isolation has been a way of life for the Castilians for so long that
they are reluctant to accept new ideas or life-styles. Yet they are
realists, facing the fact that life is a succession of long, hard labors.

*Andalusians.* The people of Andalusia in southern Spain are
characterized by manners and outlooks acquired from the Moors.
In contrast to Spaniards from the north, the typical Andalusian
has dark eyes and a well-tanned look. Since the first invading
armies of Moors came to Spain without women, they eventually
married Spanish girls who bore children with some of these
Arabian characteristics. In manner, they reflect some of the
sensuousness and volatile emotions of the Moors.

*Native dancers in La Mancha (left). Canary Islanders doing laundry (right)*

Much of the nature of the Andalusians is evident in their love of singing and in their native music. Differing entirely from the songs of other regions, the *cante jondo* ("profound song") is among the most popular. Andalusians have great appreciation for other forms of music, as well as for fine art, the dance, and literature.

*Canary Islanders.* As might be expected, the people who inhabit the seven major islands of the Canary Archipelago are as far apart from other Spaniards as their capital is from Madrid. Their very way of life, casual and unhurried, is something to be envied. Because they have suffered little from invasions, despotism, or discrimination, they are hospitable and courteous to strangers and neighbors alike. Their preference is for the simple life, as uncomplicated as possible.

Socializing is part of the way of life in the Canaries. It may vary all the way from having breakfast together at a local cafe before work to having a rousing good time at a fiesta. Canary Islanders

*The town of Vager de la Frontera, in Andalusia*

like company. Most families have household pets, a term that loosely includes barnyard animals as well as dogs, cats, birds, and tropical fish. Eating is one of the most welcome pleasures. There are plentiful supplies of fresh fruits and vegetables, shellfish, deepwater fish, poultry, and pork. Most families have a variety of favorite recipes, some local and some from other regions of Spain.

These are some of the people of Spain, and yet they are but examples. Trying to describe the Spanish people as a whole is like trying to depict an immense patchwork quilt by copying one of its tiny squares. "There remains always the intangible bedrock of Spanish character, the element of Spanishness, of *hispanidad*," wrote Dr. John A. Crow, an authority on Hispanic culture. "Perhaps the essence of the country can be found in its austere strength, its permanent vitality, but this too is an elusive quality. Whatever, wherever it is, the unity of Spain stands forth only as a vital structure of history, the sharing of a common destiny."

Spain is indeed a multitude of lands, a multitude of peoples.

# MAP KEY

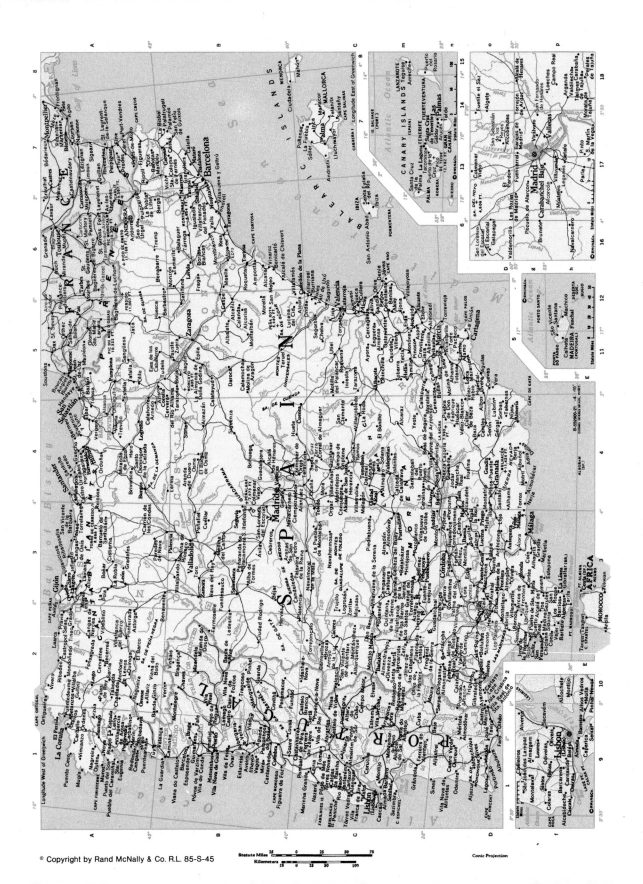

Statute Miles
Kilometers

Conic Projection

# MINI-FACTS AT A GLANCE

## GENERAL INFORMATION

**Official Name:** The Kingdom of Spain

**Capital:** Madrid

**Official Language:** Spanish

**Other Languages:** Catalan, Basque, and Galician

**Government:** Spain is a parliamentary monarchy with a constitution that was approved in 1978. The king, who is the head of the government, after consultation with majority party members suggests the appointment of the prime minister; if the latter obtains a majority of votes of the Congress of Deputies, then the king appoints him. Following suggestions of the prime minister, other members of the Council of Ministers are appointed, including the deputy premier, minister of finance and commerce, and other cabinet members. The legislature, called the Cortes Generales, has two houses—the Congress of Deputies, with 350 members, and the Senate, with 257 members. All serve four-year terms.

There are fifty provinces in Spain with their own legislatures and governors. Also, there are regional governments. For example, there are Basque, Catalan, Galician, and Andalusian parliaments.

Juan Carlos I has been king of Spain since the death of General Francisco Franco in 1975. In 1969 he had been sworn in as the official successor to Franco. Franco, who was a dictator and not part of a royal family, had ruled Spain since 1936 because he had been the military leader of the faction that won the Spanish civil war.

**Flag:** The flag has three horizontal stripes, two of red and one of yellow. The yellow stripe is half as wide as the red ones. The coat of arms is also on the flag.

**National Song:** *"Marcha real"*

**Coat of Arms:** The symbols of the shield on the coat of arms represent Aragon, Castile, and other kingdoms that became modern Spain.

**Religion:** Most Spaniards are Roman Catholics, but there is no state religion. There are a few Protestants in the country.

**Money:** The monetary unit is the peseta. The exchange rate as of July, 1985, was 162 pesetas to the United States dollar.

**Weights and Measures:** The metric system is used.

116

**Population:** 38,865,000 (1983 estimate)

**Cities** (1981 census figures):

| | |
|---|---:|
| Madrid | 3,188,297 |
| Barcelona | 1,754,900 |
| Valencia | 751,734 |
| Seville | 653,833 |
| Zaragoza (Saragossa) | 590,750 |

## GEOGRAPHY

**Highest Point:** Mount Teide, 12,162 ft. (3,707 m)

**Coastline:** 2,345 mi. (3,773 km)

**Mountains:** Much of the perimeter of the country is distinguished by high mountain ranges, rugged outcroppings, cliffs, and escarpments. The Pyrenees run east and west, from the Bay of Biscay to the Mediterranean, and serve as a barrier between Spain and France. The central high plateau is also crisscrossed by mountain ranges, some of which exceed 10,000 feet (3,048 meters). Spain is second only to Switzerland in having the highest mean elevation in western Europe.

**Climate:** The Spanish climate is as varied as the differences between northern Maine and southern Texas. The central regions have very hot summers, cold winters, and dry weather. Albacete, in the southeast of the interior plateau, has an average temperature of 40° F. (4° C) in the winter and 75° F. (24° C) in the summer. The rainfall in this region is under 15 inches (38 centimeters). Northern Spain has more moderate temperatures as well as more rainfall. La Coruña, in the northwest, has temperatures that range from an average of 48° F. (9° C) in the winter to 64° F. (18° C) in the summer. The rainfall is about 38 inches (96.5 centimeters) per year.

**Greatest Distances:** East to west—646 mi. (1,039 km)
North to south—547 mi. (880 km)

**Area:** 194,885 sq. mi. (504,772 km²), including the Balearic and Canary islands

## NATURE

**Vegetation:** In northern Spain, there are deciduous forests and meadows as well as agricultural crops such as apples and corn. The northern plateau and Ebro Valley are known for grain; the upper Ebro Valley, the southern plateau, Andalusia, and the eastern regions grow olives and grapes. Valencia and parts of Murcia are famous for citrus fruits, especially oranges; palms and olive trees grow along the Mediterranean coast. Oaks, chestnuts, elms, and pines grow along the Atlantic. The dry interior regions have ilex and cork trees and drought-resistant shrubs and plants that also can be found in American deserts.

**Fish:** There are many varieties of fish and shellfish off the coast of Spain, particularly in the Atlantic and the Bay of Biscay.

**Animals:** Wolves and bears live in the Pyrenees and in parts of the northern mountains. Deer, wild pigs, and the Spanish ibex are found in preserves, although a few Spanish ibex still can be found in the wild in the Picos de Europa mountain range. There are partridges, grouse, ducks, and rabbits throughout Spain.

## EVERYDAY LIFE

**Food:** Fish and seafood are basic to a Spaniard's diet. One of the most popular dishes in Spain is *paella*. It consists of shrimp, lobster, chicken, ham, and vegetables mixed with rice and seasoned with saffron. Squid, crabs, sardines, and fried baby eels are also very popular, as is *gazpacho*, a cold vegetable soup made of tomatoes, cucumbers, green peppers, olive oil, and spices. For those who can afford meat, which is very expensive in Spain, chicken, goat, lamb, and pork are favorites. Almost every Spaniard drinks wine with most meals except breakfast. Other drinks also favored include strong coffee and soft drinks.

**Housing:** Most city dwellers live in apartments, and in many cases own them. Most of these homes have electricity and television sets. In the country, most homes are made of clay and stone and have sloping tile roofs. The clay and stone are covered with whitewashed plaster. This covering protects the inhabitants from the harsh rays of the sun. Unlike homes in other parts of Europe, many Spanish houses are built right up to the street or sidewalk. Instead of backyards, they have courtyards enclosed by high walls.

**Holidays:**

> New Year's Day, January 1
> Epiphany, January 6
> Saint Joseph's Day, March 19
> Maundy Thursday (except Barcelona)
> Good Friday
> Easter Monday (Barcelona and Palma de Mallorca only)
> Saint Joseph the Workman's Day, May 1
> Saint Isidro's Day (Madrid only)
> Corpus Christi Day
> King Juan Carlos's Saint's Day, June 24
> Santiago de Compostela's Day, July 25
> Assumption Day
> Day of the Hispanidad (except Barcelona), October 12 (Discovery of America by Columbus)
> All Saints' Day, November 1
> Feast of the Immaculate Conception (except Barcelona), December 8
> Christmas Day, December 25
> Boxing Day (Barcelona and Palma de Mallorca only), December 26

**Culture:** Spain has a long history of artistic expression, beginning with drawings of cavemen. Spanish art bears the influence of the Celts, Phoenicians, Greeks, Romans, Carthaginians, Moors, French, and other peoples who passed through this "crossroads" of western Europe.

The Roman occupation of Spain beginning in the third century B.C., heralded a period when art and architecture began to flourish. Examples of early Roman architecture still stand in Spain.

The Moors, who began to invade Spain from North Africa at the beginning of the eighth century, also introduced new art forms. The dominant medium for Arabic artistic expression was architecture. Moorish architecture is characterized by the horseshoe arch and mosaics. Outstanding examples of Moorish art can be found in Toledo, Zaragoza, and Córdoba.

Romanesque architecture, which was simpler than the Moorish, became dominant in the late Middle Ages. It was at this time that religious art took a commanding position in Spain. The people who built Romanesque churches also commissioned paintings depicting the lives of the saints and other religious subjects. Gothic architecture was another important style, particularly evident in churches. The interiors of Gothic churches are elaborately sculptured; there are paintings everywhere.

Spanish art and architecture blossomed in the Spanish Renaissance in the sixteenth century. One of the greatest painters of this era was Domenikos Theotokopoulous, known simply as El Greco (The Greek).

The Baroque period followed the Renaissance, and religious art still remained dominant. Francisco de Zurbarán was one of the outstanding painters of the seventeenth century. He was a contemporary of another great painter—Velázquez. Other noted Spanish artists of the seventeenth and eighteenth centuries were Murillo and Goya.

The greatest figure in modern Spanish art was Pablo Picasso. Picasso was the only artist to have his work hung in the Louvre during his lifetime. Other modern Spanish artists of note are Juan Gris, José Gutiérrez Solana, Joan Miró, and Salvador Dalí.

Spanish literature existed long before the Spanish language. For almost one thousand years, literary figures in Spain were Roman and wrote in Latin. Included in this group were Seneca, Lucan, Martial, and Quintilian. As late as the tenth and eleventh centuries, outstanding work was written in the native tongues of Moslems and Jews, who lived in the southern and central regions of the country.

The first major work in the Spanish language was *El Poema de Mío Cid (Poem of the Cid)*, written in the thirteenth century.

Early Spanish literature was full of legends and epics from other countries. Arabic stories were popular, as were legends of King Arthur, Charlemagne, and the classical heroes of the Greeks and Romans.

The last half of the sixteenth century and most of the seventeenth was an era known as the Golden Age of art and architecture. The best-known book of this era was the novel *Don Quixote de la Mancha*, written by Miguel de Cervantes.

The Golden Age saw the development of early Spanish drama. Major playwrights of the era include Lope de Vega Carpio and Calderón de la Barca.

Following the Golden Age, there were very few writers of note for more than a century. By the middle of the nineteenth century, Spain was influenced by the Romantic movement in literature that was popular in England and France.

At the beginning of the twentieth century, Spanish literature was adversely affected by the nation's loss in the Spanish-American War and the decline of the Spanish Empire. One positive reaction was the birth of a movement known as *modernismo* (modernism). Two of the most influential members of the *modernismo* movement were Rubén Darío (born in Nicaragua) and Juan Ramón Jiménez.

During the 1930s and 1940s, many of Spain's best writers lived outside the country, because of the adverse political atmosphere. Some writers, such as García Lorca, Manuel Machado, and Miguel Hernández, were banned. The most renowned Spanish author of modern times is Federico García Lorca.

**Sports and Recreation:** Soccer is the most popular sport in Spain. Bullfighting is also very popular; most cities have at least one bullring.

**Communication:** Spain had little freedom of the press until recently. News media have traditionally been under state control since the Middle Ages. In recent years, however, press censorship has been abolished. Freedom of thought, belief, and expression are guaranteed by the constitution of 1978. There are about 115 daily newspapers. The largest is Madrid's *ABC*. Other large dailies include *Ya, El Pais*, and *La Vanguardia*. All of these papers can be purchased outside their home cities, but they are not truly national newspapers.

The government controls all radio and television broadcasting. In 1983, there were an estimated 10,400,000 radio sets and almost 10,000,000 television sets in Spain. In 1981, there were almost 4,000 movie theaters in the country.

**Transportation:** The network of roads and other transportation systems radiates from Madrid, in the center of the country. Kilometers are counted from the Puerta del Sol, in the center of Madrid. The main highway system consists of almost 100,000 miles (160,900 kilometers) of first-class roads.

The railroads are not as extensive as the motor highways, covering only a total of over 12,000 miles (19,308 kilometers). Most are electrified. Railroads are limited in many regions, providing service only to major cities and resorts.

Air transportation has improved greatly after being neglected until the middle 1960s. Government-owned Iberia Air Lines, which is Spain's only international airline, flies in Spain as well as in North and South America and western Europe. Many domestic flights are handled by AVIACO Airlines, also a government-owned company. There are forty-three airports in the country which cater to civilian traffic.

Inland waterway travel is negligible. But Spain has about two hundred seaports. The busiest ports are Cartagena, Santa Cruz de Tenerife, Las Palmas de Gran Canaria, Barcelona, and Bilbao.

**Education:** All Spanish children must attend school between the ages of six and fourteen. Children who do not go on to secondary schools must take vocational training between the ages of fifteen and sixteen. Secondary education is a three-year program. An additional year of study is required for students going on to a university.

Spain has over thirty universities and several technical institutions of higher learning.

**Health:** There is a universal health insurance program in Spain, which means that all Spaniards have health services.

**Principal Products:**
*Agriculture:* Wheat, barley, corn, potatoes, tomatoes, onions, apples, oranges, mandarins, almonds, grapes, cattle, pigs, sheep, poultry
*Manufacturing:* Shipbuilding, automobiles, cement, chemical products, steel, clothing, shoes

## IMPORTANT DATES

about 3000 B.C. — Iberians migrate to northeastern Spain

1000s B.C. — Phoenicians colonize Spain

about 900 B.C. — Celts invade what is modern Spain

about 600 B.C. — Second Celtic invasion of Spain

200s B.C. — Carthaginians conquer much of Spain

A.D. 61 — Saint James brings Christianity to Spain

400s — Visigoths take over Spain

711-718 — Moors conquer Spain

1000s — Christians begin to drive the Moors from Spain

1479 — Aragon and Castile unite; beginnings of modern Spanish state

1492 — Spaniards conquer Granada, the last Moorish stronghold in Spain; Columbus sails to the New World

1512 — Spaniards conquer the Kingdom of Navarre, thus uniting all of what becomes modern Spain

1513 — Núñez de Balboa reaches the Pacific Ocean

1522 — Magellan's ship completes the circumnavigation of the world

1519 — Hernán Cortés establishes a foothold in Mexico

1531 — Francisco Pizarro conquers the Inca in Peru

1588 — The English defeat the Spanish Armada

1700s—Spain is ruled by the Bourbon dynasty

1763—Spain and France are defeated by England in the Seven Years' War

1776—Spain supports the thirteen American colonies against England

1779—War between Spain and England

1808—Napoleon Bonaparte invades Spain; Carlos IV, the Spanish king, is forced to abdicate in favor of Joseph Bonaparte, Napoleon's brother

1813—The French are driven out of Spain

1814—Ferdinand VII is restored to the throne

1810-1825—Most of Spain's colonies proclaim their independence

1833-1839—Civil war in Spain

1898—Spanish–American War

1909-1926—Spain and France try to establish a protectorate in Morocco

1931—Alfonso XIII is deposed; the Second Republic is formed

1936-1939—Spanish civil war

1942—General Francisco Franco revives the Cortes (legislative assembly)

1947—Franco announces that the monarchy will be restored after his death or retirement

1967—First election since the Spanish civil war; a portion of the Cortes is elected

1969—Franco nominates Prince Juan Carlos de Borbón as his successor

1973—Franco names Luis Carrero Blanco president of Council of Ministers

1973—Carrero Blanco is assassinated and Carlos Arias Navarro succeeds him

1975—Franco dies; Prince Juan Carlos becomes king

1976—Restrictions on political activity are lifted; Arias Navarro resigns his post and is succeeded by Adolfo Suárez González

1977—General elections for the Cortes

1978—New constitution establishes Spain as a parliamentary monarchy

1979—General elections; new government headed by Adolfo Suárez

1980—Basque and Catalan parliaments elected

1981—Suárez resigns; Leopoldo Calvo Sotelo, also a centrist, is nominated to succeed him; attempted coup; Calvo Sotelo forms a new Council of Ministers

1982—Felipe González Márquez, a Socialist, forms a new Council of Ministers

## IMPORTANT PEOPLE

Isaac Albéniz (1860-1909), composer, founder of contemporary Spanish music

Alfonso XIII (1886-1941), king of Spain who was deposed with the establishment of the Second Republic

Joseph Bonaparte (1768-1844), king of Naples (from 1806) and Spain (1808-1813), brother of Napoleon I, known in Spain as "Pepe Botella" ("Bottle Joe") because of his heavy drinking

Juan Boscán Almogáver (c. 1495-1542), poet

Pedro Calderón de la Barca (1600-1681), historical and philosophical playwright

Don Carlos (1788-1855), brother of Ferdinand VII and pretender to the throne

Carlos III (1716-1788), king of Spain, Parma, and Naples

Carlos IV (1784-1819), king who was forced to abdicate the throne by Napoleon

Miguel de Cervantes (1547-1616), novelist, author of *Don Quixote de la Mancha*

Christopher Columbus (1451-1506), Italian explorer who discovered the New World for Spain

Hernán Cortés (1458-1547), conqueror of Mexico

Salvador Dalí (1904- ), surrealist painter

George Dewey (1837-1917), American admiral who destroyed Spanish fleet at Manila

Sir Francis Drake (1540?-1596), English admiral, defeated Spanish Armada

José Echegaray (1833-1916), scientist and playwright, won Nobel Prize in literature in 1904

Elizabeth I (1533-1603), English queen during whose reign the Spanish Armada was defeated by the English

Manuel de Falla (1876-1946), modern Spanish composer

Ferdinand III (1199-1252), king who conquered Seville in 1248

Ferdinand VII (1784-1833), king restored to throne after Napoleon's defeat

Francisco Franco (1892-1975), Spanish dictator from 1936 to 1975

Federico García Lorca (1899-1936), poet and playwright

Luis de Góngora (1561-1627), poet of the Golden Age

Francisco Goya (1746-1828), one of the greatest Spanish artists

Enrique Granados (1867-1916), composer of *Twelve Spanish Dances* and *Goyescas*

El Greco (Domenikos Theotokopoulous; 1541-1614), Spanish artist

Juan Gris (José Victoriano; 1887-1927), modern artist

José Gutiérrez Solana (1886-1945), artist who based his work on the masters

Hasdrubal (died 207 B.C.), Carthaginian leader

Miguel Hernández (1910-1942), great lyric poet

Juan de Herrera (1530-1597), architect under Philip II, who designed Philip's palace, El Escorial

Washington Irving (1783-1859), American novelist, author of *Tales of the Alhambra* and an attaché at the American embassy in Madrid

Isabella I (1451-1504), wife of Ferdinand II of Aragon, queen of Castile and sponsor of Columbus

Isabella II (1830-1904), queen of Spain, abdicated in favor of son Alfonso XII

Saint James (Santiago; died A.D. 62), man who brought Christianity to Spain

Juan Ramón Jiménez (1881-1958), lyric poet, won Nobel Prize in literature in 1959

Juan Carlos (1938-    ), present king of Spain

Mariano Jose de Larra (1809-1837), great satirist of the nineteenth century

Lucan (39-65), Roman poet (Marcus Annaeus Lucanus)

Manuel Machado (1874-1947), poet, playwright

Ferdinand Magellan (1480-1521), Portuguese navigator

Martial (Marcus Valerius Martialis; c. 40-102), Roman writer

Joan Miró (1893-    ), Catalonian abstract painter

Bartolomé Esteban Murillo (1618-82), painter

Vasco Núñez de Balboa (1475-1519), explorer, discovered Pacific Ocean

Philip II (1527-98), king and the most powerful monarch of his day; the Spanish Armada was defeated during his reign

Philip III (1578-1621), king of Spain

Philip IV (1605-1665), king of Spain

Pablo Picasso (1881-1973), the most famous modern Spanish painter

Francisco Pizarro (1471-1541), conqueror of Peru

Miguel Primo de Rivera (1870-1930), dictator, 1925-30

Quintilian (Marcus Fabius Quintilianus; 1st century A.D.), Roman writer

Santiago Ramón y Cajal (1852-1934), physician specializing in histology; won Noble Prize in medicine in 1906

Roderick (Rodrigo; died 713), last Visigoth king of Spain

Seneca (Lucius Annaeus; 4 B.C.-A.D. 65), Roman statesman and philosopher, born in Córdoba, Spain

Diego Rodriguez de Silva y Velázquez (1599-1660), great painter

Garcilaso de la Vega (1503-1536), army captain and poet, wrote the "Eglogas"

Francisco de Zurbarán (1598-1664), seventeenth-century religious painter

# INDEX

**Page numbers that appear in boldface type indicate illustrations**

## About the Authors

Wilbur Cross, a professional writer and editor, is the author of some 25 non-fiction books and several hundred magazine articles. His subjects range widely from travel and foreign culture to history, sociology, medicine, business, adventure, biography, humor, education, and politics. Mr. Cross worked for several years as a copywriter and was an associate editor at *Life* magazine.

Esther Cross has assisted her husband with numerous books and magazine articles. She coauthored with him *A Guide to Unusual Vacations*, covering interesting locations in the United States. Most of her time now is devoted to real estate, being a partner in a Bronxville, New York, firm.

The Crosses have traveled extensively in Latin America and Europe, including Spain and Portugal. The parents of four daughters, they live in Westchester County, New York.